"Finding a book specific to OCD within the framework of ACT is a long-awaited victory. At last! A book for people like me. The book is a delightful read, written in a helpful, concise way that makes a life with OCD seem possible, even hopeful. It felt like a lifeline to me, giving me the desire to keep going and keep finding the joy."

—Brittany H.

"*Imperfectly Good* by Annabella Hagen is a lucid and pragmatic guide for people of any faith tradition or of no faith who, like myself, are learning to manage life with scrupulosity OCD. It is written for those who wish to live the values that "make their heart sing" no matter what they fear or what their rule-based scrupulosity-OCD mind may be telling them. The exercises in this companion manual will help you develop the skills you need to see your internal experiences from a different perspective so you can more truly and flexibly live and find joy in the values that matter most to you."

—Brewster Fay, PhD

"Highly recommended! Based on principles of ACT, this is an accessible guide to help scrupulous individuals choose a path toward the things they value instead of chasing anxiety relief and ironically finding themselves more stuck in the scrupulosity trap. Along with a therapist, this book can help you develop psychological flexibility and learn to let go of fear and find peace."

—Jedidiah Siev, PhD

"This is honestly one of my new favorite resources for use in the world of faith, OCD, and religious scrupulosity. I deeply appreciate the way Annabella simultaneously helped readers understand their scrupulosity, offer themselves compassion, and move towards their authentic faith in a value-driven way. Many of her metaphors helped to reframe my own understanding of OCD, and I can't wait to share this groundbreaking resource with the wider community!"

—Rev. Katie O'Dunne, Founder, Faith & Mental Health Integrative Service

"*Imperfectly Good* is a fantastic resource for anyone with scrupulosity. It reflects the most up-to-date information and treatment strategies that you need to be guided by faith, not fear!"

—Jonathan S. Abramowitz, PhD

"Readers are certain to find tools that will be useful to them in their healing journey."
—Debra Theobald McClendon, PhD, Licensed Psychologist

Imperfectly Good

Other Books by Annabella Hagen

The Masterpiece Mindset:
Empowering Your Kids to be Confident, Compassionate, and Resilient
(coauthored with Dave Hagen)

Let Go of Anxiety:
Climb Life's Mountains with Peace, Purpose, and Resilience

Imperfectly Good

Navigating Religious and Moral Anxiety to Release Fear and Find Peace

Annabella Hagen, LCSW

Mindset
Family Therapy

Copyright © 2022 by Annabella Hagen

All rights reserved, including the right to reproduce this workbook, or portions thereof, in any form. No part of this workbook may be used or reproduced in any manner whatsoever without written permission from the publisher, except in the case of brief quotations embodied in critical articles and reviews. The views expressed herein are the responsibility of the author and do not necessarily represent the position of the publisher. For information or permission, visit MindsetFamilyTherapy.com, mindsetfamilytherapy@gmail.com, or call (801) 427-1054.

This is a work of creative nonfiction. The events herein are portrayed to the best of the author's memory. While all the stories in this workbook are true, some names and identifying details may have been changed to protect the privacy of the people involved.

Cover design by MiblArt
Interior print design and layout by Marny K. Parkin
Ebook design and layout by Marny K. Parkin
Wave image by hati.royani | Vecteezy.com

Mindset Family Therapy
Published by Mindset Family Therapy
ISBN 978-0-9973210-6-7

You can enjoy life's journey even when the scrupulous mind is present. To continue moving toward your values, go to mindsetfamilytherapy.com and find more practices you can download. You can also sign up for my monthly newsletter and get access to evidence-based skills training to continue to be open, aware, and engaged in what matters most to you.

To everyone out there who is struggling with religious and moral anxiety (scrupulosity OCD). You are my inspiration, and this book is for you!

Contents

Introduction		1
1	Religious and Moral Anxiety: Seeing the Big Picture	5
2	Doing What Matters Most to You	24
3	Understanding the Mind	33
4	Recognizing Your Internal Experiences	49
5	Learning to Defuse from Internal Experiences	68
6	Being Open to Uncertainty	75
7	Taking What's Being Offered Now	89
8	Addressing Dilemmas of Faith	105
9	Connecting to the Present Moment	115
10	Being Aware of Being Aware	127
11	Developing Self-Forgiveness and Self-Compassion	135
12	Staying on the Path Less Traveled	147
13	Being Willing to Do What It Takes	152
14	Stepping into the River	156
15	Going Beyond What You See	195

Epilogue	200
Frequently Asked Questions	203
Notes	208
Note to the Reader	215
What's Next?	216
About the Author	217

Introduction

Treating anxiety disorders and obsessive-compulsive disorder became personal for me years before I became a psychotherapist. Unbeknownst to my husband and me, our youngest son's early childhood stubborn streaks were an indication of his anxiety challenges. By the time he was in elementary school, his "just so" behaviors were evident, but we hoped he would grow out of them. By middle school, we realized he needed professional help.

Long story short, we literally "took the tour" around the different cities in our state in search of a therapist who knew how to treat anxiety disorders and OCD, to no avail. It wasn't until our son was in his early twenties that he himself found a specialist from California. Eda Gorbis and her intensive outpatient treatment made a significant difference in his life.

Our experience motivated me to become appropriately trained at the Behavior Therapy Training Institute sponsored by the International IOCD Foundation. My aim was to get specialty training so other families in my state wouldn't have to experience the frustration we did in trying to find someone who understood and knew how to treat anxiety disorders and OCD.

Since then, I've worked with many of those who struggle with religious and moral anxiety. They, and you, are my inspiration for writing this workbook. Before seeking treatment, those struggling with this anxiety will often go to their faith leaders for answers. After meeting with these spiritual leaders, many will feel "reassured." Unfortunately, soon after, their anxiety and uncertainty are back in full force.

In confusion, they often ask, "Why can't I live my religion perfectly? Why is my faith causing me such torment? Maybe I didn't tell my faith leader everything. I need to talk to them again." Sometimes they just try to power through and abide by the tenets of their religion. Sometimes they take a break or abandon their faith altogether, hoping to find peace. Unfortunately, their anxiety and doubt about their moral decisions are still there.

Eventually, through friends, relatives, and internet searches, they find out that their anxiety related to their faith and values actually has a name: scrupulosity obsessive-compulsive disorder. They feel great relief to learn it has a name and that treatment is available.

The International OCD Foundation knows that many throughout the world suffer in silence because there is not enough awareness of this type of OCD. **Please check out their website at https://iocdf.org/ocdandfaith/ for more information.**

I hope this workbook contributes to an increasing awareness for those suffering with this challenge as well as for their loved ones and spiritual leaders, regardless of denomination.

I also hope it will help you understand that though you may be imperfectly good, it is possible to navigate religious and moral anxiety so you can release fear and find peace!

This workbook includes principles and skills founded upon acceptance and commitment therapy (ACT), an evidence-based form of psychotherapy derived from cognitive and behavioral therapies and other universal principles Steve Hayes and colleagues have researched since the 1980s and continue to research.

It also includes exposure and response-prevention (ERP)[1] skills—the behavior part of cognitive-behavioral therapy (CBT). ERP is the gold-standard treatment for OCD, including religious and moral anxiety, or scrupulosity OCD.

You'll see ERP principles throughout this workbook because ACT is an exposure-based model and has ERP built into it. ACT has been shown to be effective in promoting and enhancing the success of ERP in individuals struggling with OCD.[2] Chapter 15 includes specific instructions for conducting exposures and applying ACT principles as you choose to live a values-focused life.

As you clear your mind of the noise you may experience in the form of thoughts, feelings, sensations, urges, and other internal experiences, you will be able to get back to living a rich and meaningful life and, most importantly, find joy in your faith and values as you continue your unique journey.

How to Read and Apply the Skills Taught in This Workbook

This is your journey, and this workbook is designed to help you along that journey. As with any other workbook, you may initially feel overwhelmed or frustrated. It may at times feel like you need to do each exercise before you can move on to the next. You may want to just "get to the finish line and be cured." This is normal when you are looking for answers to your pain and suffering.

The following suggestions may help you in the process.

First, Browse the Workbook All the Way Through

I invite you to skim the entire workbook with curiosity to get a big picture of what you'll be doing before you start the real work. Once you have a sense of it, go back and start reading thoroughly and applying the skills.

What Matters Most to You?

Most likely, you've chosen to read this workbook because your anxious mind is targeting what you value most—your spirituality and values. Pay special attention to chapter 2, which addresses what matters most in your life. What you want your life to be about will be your beacon as you read and implement the skills found in this workbook.

Triggers

Triggers are basically opportunities to respond to stimuli. These stimuli can be anything in your environment (people, places, pets, words, sounds, etc.) or internal experiences, such as thoughts or feelings. Anything that brings about, produces, or generates the urge to worry excessively is a trigger and can lead you to become stuck.

As you read this workbook, make a note of where you're being triggered. If you need to, take a break from that particular section and move on. Come back to it when you are ready. Little by little, as you start applying the principles and skills found herein, you'll discover you are able to keep reading even when there is discomfort.

Remember, you are reading this workbook so you can release fear and find peace. Don't let the anxious mind tell you that you can't do it.

Exposures

Exposures are not just about facing your fears and white-knuckling it through life. You already do that every day. The purpose of exposures is to help you change your relationship with any external (e.g., watching a movie) or internal (e.g., thought, judgment, memory, feeling, sensation, urge) experiences you happen upon as you strive to live a meaningful life.

As you learn how to become open, aware, and actively engaged in what really matters to you (e.g., being caring, grateful, connecting with others), you'll be more flexible and able to respond differently than you currently are. You will be able to acknowledge, describe, and accept those internal events—thoughts, memories, feelings, sensations, and urges—as such.

Life is full of surprises. This workbook will help you learn to live with resilience, hope, peace and flexibility, even when the anxious mind spews out unhelpful advice. Please note that the examples I use to give you an idea what your mind might say, or what you might say to your mind, are just that—examples, springboards to get you thinking. Please feel free to come up with your own statements and questions in these situations.

Metaphors and Stories

I share metaphors and stories designed to help you in your learning. If you can't relate to all of them, that's okay. Not everyone will identify with each of the stories and metaphors. Use those that resonate with you and add and substitute your own stories and metaphors.

Find a Treatment Provider

This workbook is just that—a workbook. It's not a substitute for psychotherapy. If you are not currently working with a treatment provider, please find one who can tailor your treatment to your needs. The International OCD Foundation lists providers who have been appropriately trained to treat OCD, and it does so by state. **Here is the link: https://iocdf.org/ocd-finding-help/.**

You will also notice that throughout this workbook, I emphasize and reemphasize certain principles and themes. Developing mental flexibility requires knowledge, action, and repetition. Learning takes time and patience. Becoming is a process.

You're about to learn how to respond to your mind in a way that's different from what you have done in the past so you can start focusing on what matters most in your life.

Are you ready? Let's do this!

1
Religious and Moral Anxiety: Seeing the Big Picture

The details seem so important and so necessary—and indeed they are, but not to the point that they deprive us of peace. Balance is required, and therein lies the real struggle.

—Father Thomas M. Santa

Amber's Story

Amber was an agnostic with high morals. Unfortunately, she often questioned her motivations regarding her behaviors and values. "Did I really mean to give that donation, or is it my savior complex? What if God really exists and I am sinning by not believing? Did I inadvertently offend my co-workers yesterday?" She seemed determined to be perfectly good, and was harsh on herself when she realized she failed at it every time.

Relatives and friends would provide reassurance to help her feel better, but it never really worked. It wasn't until she searched for her symptoms on the internet that she found answers. She was surprised and relieved to know there was actually a name for her emotional challenges—scrupulosity obsessive-compulsive disorder.

How about you? Are you surprised? There are many individuals, including medical and mental health providers, who haven't heard of this kind of anxiety as a subtype of OCD.

If you didn't know that the incessant anxiety and uncertainty related to your faith and moral beliefs are linked to scrupulosity OCD, this chapter will help you better understand this condition. If you already know you have OCD, this chapter will review and clarify some relevant concepts for you.

Obsessive-Compulsive Disorder (OCD)

The Doubting Illness

OCD has been called "the doubting disease." Uncertainty is the driving force behind it. Your worries and fears (i.e., your obsessions) target the things that matter most to you. You may constantly obsess about the past or future. The need to know the consequences of your fears leads you to immerse yourself in repetitive "safety" behaviors or rituals (compulsions), like ruminating or seeking reassurance from others. OCD leads you to doubt yourself and to believe that you are the exception to the rule. The more you doubt you have OCD, the more likely it is that you have it.

No matter what the mind comes up with, it's never enough to satisfy the uncertainty you feel. You try to use logic, but you are caught in what feels like a trap. Your incessant doubts can feel unbearable and are often painful. You wish you had the *absolute* answer and could move on with your life.

Misconceptions

The presence of anxiety alone does not mean someone has obsessive-compulsive disorder. While a person may exhibit signs of OCD, to determine whether they actually have OCD, we must consider the degree of disruption to their life.

Some may excessively check the locks, the stove, or the appliances to make sure there won't be a fire or robbery. These are the types of repetitive OCD rituals most people can easily identify with. However, it is not always obvious when someone has OCD because they may neutralize their excessive worries (obsessions) with additional thoughts to relieve those worries.

And because it is often misunderstood, OCD can go undiagnosed. It has been reported that it takes an average of fourteen to seventeen years from the time OCD symptoms show up before a person gets adequate professional help.[1] Loved ones, spiritual leaders, and even the clients themselves often don't realize their excessive thinking and feelings of uncertainty may actually indicate a clinical condition.

A Genetic Predisposition

Studies[2] show that genetic factors play a role in the development of OCD. While some people may have close relatives (e.g., parents and siblings) who struggle with OCD, others report they are the only ones struggling with the disorder. However, this latter group reports having family members who are challenged by other mental health conditions, such as anxiety and depression. It is not clear why some individuals end up with the disorders when their family members don't.

A Neurological Condition

Research shows that the basal ganglia and other structures in the brain, such as the orbital cortex, striatum, caudate nucleus, and thalamus,[3] are affected in those who suffer from obsessive-compulsive disorder. Communication between these structures is critical. With OCD, this communication is disrupted. Some of the neurotransmitters or chemical messengers (i.e., serotonin and dopamine) that aid this communication are also involved.

A Behavioral Challenge

When you experience painful thoughts that don't align with the person you are or want to be, you may feel you need to change something, which leads you to engage in safety behaviors (compulsions) in an attempt to find mental, emotional, and physical relief. The more you give in to these behaviors, the stronger the compulsions become, making OCD a behavioral disorder.

Measuring the Severity of OCD

The degree to which people experience OCD varies widely. The Y-BOCS (Yale-Brown Obsessive-Compulsive Scale) measures the severity of the illness. If you wish to determine the severity of your OCD, you can ask your treatment provider for the Y-BOCS or find it on the internet.

What Does OCD Look Like?

In short, there are two aspects of the OCD experience: the **obsessions** (your ongoing anxious and fearful thoughts) and the **compulsions** (the private or public measures you take to alleviate the distress you experience because of anxious and fearful thoughts). Your life functioning is disrupted when the rituals you engage in to find relief from anxiety, uncertainty, guilt, shame, and many other emotions take over your life.

As mentioned, compulsions may be **public** (e.g., repeatedly asking your best friend if they think you are a bad person) and **private** (e.g., incessantly picking apart your thoughts to figure them out). You may also obsess about why you cannot control your thoughts and spend hours scrutinizing the answers your mind comes up with. It doesn't matter how long you search your mind for reassurance (private compulsion) or how long it takes you to find the answer on the internet (public compulsion) or in any other place; the answers can't eliminate the uncertainty and anxiety.

If someone has OCD and doesn't get appropriate treatment, the symptoms are likely to increase and become debilitating. The good news is that even though OCD is a chronic illness, it *is* treatable. You can learn to be comfortable with uncertainty and live a meaningful and values-focused life.

Types of OCD

While this workbook focuses on religious and moral anxiety (i.e., scrupulosity OCD), most who struggle with this type of OCD also deal with subsets depending on the content of their thoughts and what themes their obsessive-compulsive disorder is targeting. Below are two short lists of the most common obsessions individuals experience with other forms of OCD and the compulsions those suffering with OCD employ.

Common Obsessions and Examples of Them

- Religious (fears around having blasphemous thoughts)
- Contamination (fears around environmental contaminants)
- Losing control (fears around acting on impulses to harm others or oneself)
- Harm (fears around harming others when not careful enough)
- Sexual (fears around inappropriate sexual behavior with others)
- Superstitious or magical (excessive worry around objects and other situations)
- Health (excessive worry around physical well-being)
- Perfectionistic (questioning whether you have told the truth perfectly)
- Neutral (excessive awareness of your thought processes)

Types of Compulsions

- Mental (private) compulsions (mentally reviewing past events)
- Behavioral (public) compulsions (shaking one's head to "get rid" of a thought)
- Reassurance-seeking compulsions (these can be private or public)
- Avoidant behaviors (staying away from loved ones for fear of harming them)

For more detailed examples of the most common obsessions and compulsions, please go to this link: **https://iocdf.org/about-ocd/**.

Although OCD may bring up new worries, the tools you'll learn to use in this workbook apply to other situations related to OCD and life in general.

Please remember: you may have OCD, but OCD is not your life.

Let's take a look at the OCD cycle, which I refer to as the **"scrupulosity trap"** in this workbook.

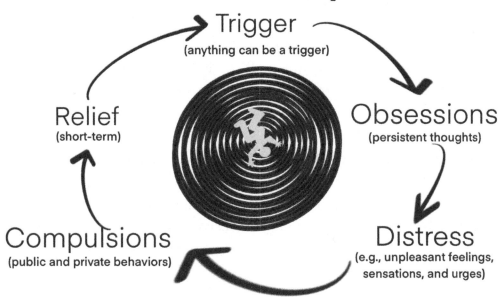

When you get stuck in the scrupulosity trap, you'll notice the following events:

- **Triggers:** Anything in your environment (people, places, pets, words, sounds, etc.) or internal experiences, such as thoughts or feelings, that bring about the urge to obsess and lead you to become stuck in the scrupulosity trap.

- **Obsessions:** Repetitive, excessive "worry thoughts" that can lead you to experience other difficult internal events.

- **Distress:** Unpleasant events, such as feelings, bodily sensations, and urges, that can feel intolerable.

    - **Feelings:** Anxiety, uncertainty, guilt, shame, etc.

    - **Bodily sensations:** Feelings manifested in your body. You may believe you cannot tolerate these sensations, which may lead you to the urge to do something about them.

    - **Urges:** You feel like you need to fix the situation (e.g., scratch an itch), since the internal experiences have become overwhelming.

- **Compulsions:** Unhelpful safety behaviors you engage in to temporarily alleviate the discomfort triggered by a situation. These behaviors can be **public** (things others see you doing, such as repetitively asking for reassurance from a loved one or reading and rereading information on the internet) or **private** (things you do internally and privately, such as figuring things out in your head, fixating on past actions, or trying to predict the future). You may also find yourself engaging in excessive avoidant behaviors to find relief from your distress.

- **Relief:** Because you may have found seconds, minutes, or perhaps even hours of relief, your anxious mind leads you to believe that if you do these behaviors more intensely or longer, you might eventually find permanent relief. This short-term relief keeps you stuck in the cycle when you get triggered again.

Awareness Build-Up

Are you aware of how often you get caught up in the scrupulosity trap? Take a few days to notice and track when you get stuck in it. At least once a day, briefly write about your experience and see if you notice any patterns. If you wish, take a picture of the OCD cycle graphic and the prompts below so you have them handy on your smartphone.

- **Trigger:** What event (internal or external) led you to get stuck?
- **Obsessions:** What thoughts did you notice? Write down at least three or four persistent thoughts you had after being triggered.
- **Distress:** What difficult internal events showed up?
    - **Feelings:** What uncomfortable feelings did you experience? Write down the strongest feelings you noticed (anxiety, uncertainty, shame, guilt, etc.).
    - **Bodily sensations:** The feelings manifested in your body can be unpleasant, and you may want to get rid of them. Where do you feel them in your body, and how do they feel?
    - **Urges:** What did you want to do to fix the situation? What did you end up doing when the distress became unbearable?
- **Compulsions (private or public):** What safety behaviors did you engage in to find some type of relief?
- **Relief:** How long did you feel the relief before you were triggered by the same event or something else?

Let's now delve into an overview of religious and moral anxiety, or scrupulosity OCD.

Scrupulosity

The word *scrupulous* comes from the Latin word *scrupulum*, which means "a small, sharp stone." In ancient Rome, a scruple was a unit of weight measurement. For our purposes, the small, sharp stone represents the persistent pain someone experiences from day to day, much like the pain from a pebble in someone's shoe, except they cannot get rid of it.[4]

When people are scrupulous, they want to be exact in the way they conduct themselves when it comes to their **religion, their morals, or both**. And their anxious mind targets the things that matter most to them. The constant need to live their morals and religion perfectly and feeling like they are falling short leads them to experience anxiety, uncertainty, and sometimes depression.

"I know others can't be perfect, but I know better! Others will be disappointed in me. I should be perfectly obedient! I've been blessed, so God expects more from me!" Does this sound familiar?

When you feel like you are not following your faith's precepts and moral beliefs, your anxious mind may insist that you have to do it perfectly. This belief may persist no matter what you do. This workbook can help you recognize that being imperfectly good is enough. You can change your relationship with the unpleasant internal experiences (e.g., anxiety and uncertainty) and find joy in what matters most to you—your values.

Is your affliction leading you to employ "safety" behaviors (confessing to your faith leader or mentally reviewing your actions, etc.) that may temporarily relieve any uncomfortable emotions?

It doesn't have to be this way. You may not have realized your ordeal has a name and that there are evidence-based treatment skills that can help you. You no longer need to suffer in silence!

Below are some of the most common obsessions and compulsions associated with religious and moral scrupulosity. Mark those you currently struggle with. As you read through these obsessions and compulsions, you may find some overlap between moral and religious OCD.

Religious Scrupulosity

Obsessions

- Fear of offending Deity (deliberately or inadvertently) with:
  - Blasphemous or sexual thoughts
  - Uncertainty about inappropriate sexual or perceived harmful behaviors
  - Not keeping your religion's principles perfectly
  - Not serving God and/or others perfectly

- Fear of having acted sinfully
- Fear of a punishing God and feeling or being condemned
- Fear that your intentions, feelings, and sensations are wrong
    - You doubt your faith and feel sinful for doing so.
    - You believe you are using OCD as an excuse for your perceived sinful thoughts.
    - You believe certain feelings and sensations are sinful (e.g., anger, sexual arousal).
- High responsibility and self-blame for your thoughts, feelings, sensations, and urges
- Fear that you may be a culprit in someone's death, or feelings of eternal doom
- Fear of sexual thoughts related to Deity or religious authorities
- Fear of being possessed by Satan and/or other evil spirits

List any additional obsessions below:

Compulsions

- Avoiding anything that triggers unwanted thoughts, feelings, sensations, and urges
- Seeking reassurance with public or private behaviors (e.g., repeatedly talking to yourself or confessing to someone to get reassurance that you wouldn't or didn't commit a certain sin, or to find relief from unwanted thoughts, feelings, and/or sensations)
- Repeating religious rituals until you feel God has listened to and accepted your prayers and/or offerings

- Engaging in behaviors that help you remember you did not do anything sinful

- Continually criticizing or inflicting physical punishment on yourself for immoral thoughts, past or future immoral misdeeds, or as "motivation" to be a better person

- Washing or bathing to "get rid of" unwanted "sinful" thoughts, feelings, and sensations

- Bargaining with the Creator to ensure forgiveness and find relief from intense guilt and other unwanted emotions

- Excessive and repetitive behaviors or thoughts (rumination) about how you can make things better or undo "bad" thoughts, feelings, sensations, and/or urges

- Continually asking God for forgiveness

- Constantly reviewing your thoughts, feelings, sensations, and urges to ensure yourself you haven't acted in opposition to your religious beliefs

- Sacrificing joy and earthly privileges to show the Supreme Being your devotion and/or repentance

List any additional compulsions below:

Moral Scrupulosity

Obsessions

- Worrying about whether you have behaved inappropriately against your ethical and moral beliefs in the various roles you have in life (e.g., as a family member, friend, neighbor, or citizen)

- Obsessing about past behaviors and whether you have inadvertently hurt someone either emotionally, physically, or financially

- Worrying about past behaviors you've resolved and questioning whether you've done enough to fix things or have missed an important part of the situation either inadvertently or purposely
- Obsessing about the possible consequences of being found out for your perceived misdeeds
- Worrying about being unworthy of respect, appreciation, and love because of past behaviors (i.e., impostor syndrome)
- Mentally replaying the different scenarios where you may have compromised your moral standards
- Continuously reviewing past experiences to "discover" whether you did more than you actually remember
- Constantly worrying about an action or lack of action that may cause harm to others in the present or the immediate or distant future
- Taking blame and emotional responsibility for others' misfortunes

List any additional moral obsessions below:

Compulsions

- Avoiding anything that triggers the unwanted thoughts, emotions, sensations, and urges that bring up uncertainty regarding your moral behavior
- Seeking reassurance that you are not as bad as your OCD mind says you are (e.g., asking loved ones, reading information, or mentally going back in time to ensure you actually didn't do anything wrong)
- Criticizing self and inflicting physical punishment for immoral thoughts or an immoral past as "motivation" to be a better person
- Ritualized words and/or behaviors that decrease anxiety, guilt, uncertainty, and other unwanted emotions and sensations related to your values

- Excessive "altruistic" behaviors that reassure you that you are a good person (though, in reality, they're appeasing the OCD demands)
- Constantly reviewing possible scenarios and preparing for the worst
- Ruminating and rationalizing to find relief from unwanted thoughts, feelings, and sensations
- Constantly reviewing your thoughts, feelings, sensations, and urges to make sure you haven't acted against your values
- Repeatedly sacrificing joy and privileges for the sake of others because you don't think you deserve happiness

List any additional moral obsessions below:

Giving in to compulsions and/or avoidant behaviors to find relief from the fear OCD brings into your life inadvertently strengthens the wrong neural pathways. These behaviors also affect your ability to be flexible with external or internal experiences (e.g., thoughts, judgments, memories, feelings, sensations, and urges), which can also influence your ability to let go of fear so you can find peace. This workbook will teach you how to develop psychological flexibility.[5]

What Is Psychological Flexibility?

AWARE
OPEN
ACTIVELY ENGAGED

- Present Moment
- Acceptance
- Values
- Psychological Flexibility
- Defusion
- Committed Action
- Observing-Self Perspective

Psychological flexibility is the ability to be open, aware, and actively engaged in what matters most to you (what you value). As you develop this flexibility, you'll find long-term vitality, hope, and peace in your life as opposed to the short-term relief you receive from repeating compulsions.

As you develop psychological flexibility, you'll become more **open** to painful internal experiences. This means you'll be able to get unstuck (**defusion**) from them and allow (**acceptance**) them to come and go without getting caught in the scrupulosity trap.

Psychological flexibility will enhance your **awareness** so you can connect with the here and now (the **present moment**) and recognize that you are aware of being aware (what we'll call the **observing-self perspective**) without having to become absorbed in compulsive and avoidant behaviors to get rid of internal events (e.g., thoughts and feelings).

As you develop psychological flexibility, you'll become **actively engaged** in what is worth (**values**) your focus, time, and energy and choose (**committed action**) to do what matters most in your life.

The Plasticity of Your Brain

Your brain can literally change its physical makeup based on the things you do. When you repeat certain behaviors, whether helpful or unhelpful, your neurons wire together and reinforce those behaviors.[6] When you continue to obsess and get stuck in the scrupulosity trap, you continually reinforce those OCD pathways.

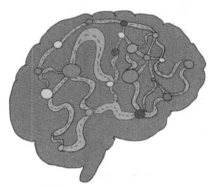

As you implement psychological-flexibility skills, you will enhance your brain's ability to change.

Learning something new—whether playing an instrument, performing a sport, or any other skill—takes practice, time, and effort. And so it is with the skills you'll learn here. The more you practice them, the more those new neural pathways will be reinforced. This is good news! Your brain can change when you start doing something different from what you've been doing.

Building New Neural Pathways

Creating new neural pathways takes time; be patient. Someone who struggles with scrupulosity OCD shared this with me:

"Compulsions (public and private) are the easiest path because they're so trodden on, and they become easier the more we do them. Forging a new path is difficult at first because there's a lot of brush to cut and tromp down, but as we continue using the new path, the old path starts to grow over. However, that doesn't mean they go away, and if we give in to a compulsion, we're reversing our progress by re-tromping down the leaves on the unwanted path."

Choosing the Path Less Traveled

Shar's Story

One day, a friend asked Shar if she could pick him up as his car had broken down near her workplace. The problem was that Shar could not just leave work at any time. She apologized, and her friend told her it was not a big deal. He had only called because he knew she worked nearby.

But Shar beat herself up the rest of the afternoon for not being there for her friend. She reasoned, "I value service and compassion, and by not serving my friend, I am not living up to my values. I need to make it up to him. I'll bring him dinner tonight." But then she remembered she had a commitment with her brother. She ruminated all afternoon to the point she was unable to concentrate on her job and couldn't enjoy visiting with her brother. She didn't realize that when she acted on the urge to be perfectly good, her private and public compulsions were in the service of her anxious mind and not in the service of her values.

The Road Not Taken

Most often than not, when clients share their challenges with OCD, I cannot help but think of the well-known verse written by Robert Frost:

> *Two roads diverged in a wood, and I—*
> *I took the one less traveled by,*
> *And that has made all the difference.*[7]

When you feel overwhelmed and stuck in the OCD cycle, it's easier to take the most frequently traveled road (graphic below). The anxious mind may say that your compulsive and avoidant behaviors are in the service of your values. Sure, they may provide short-term relief, but they won't allow you to move toward what matters most in your life.

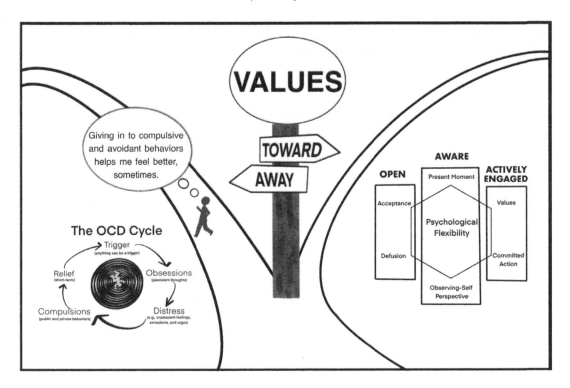

The new path is psychological flexibility.
It'll be hard but well worth it!

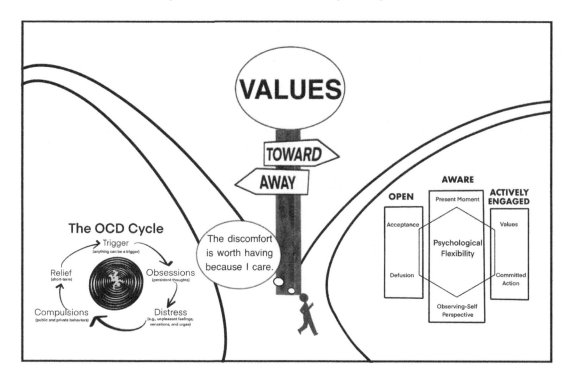

As you go about life, you can practice psychological flexibility (shown above) and take the road less traveled, creating new neural pathways in your brain. As you do, you'll begin to change your relationship with your thoughts and feelings and other internal experiences. It will take patience, effort, and time, and it will make all the difference. **You have a choice.**

Before we move on, I invite you to complete the Acceptance and Action Questionnaire–II (AAQ-II)[8] to determine where you are in terms of being open and willing to experience difficult internal events (e.g., thoughts, judgments, memories, feelings, sensations, and urges).

Add up your score for each question. The lower the total score, the more psychological flexibility you are exhibiting. The higher the total score, the less flexible you may be and living a meaningful life may be more difficult. You can also find this questionnaire at the end of this workbook. In addition to completing the questionnaire before you move on, consider completing it *after* reading and applying the skills found in this workbook. Doing so will help you track your level of mental and emotional flexibility at the different stages of your journey in changing your relationship with OCD.

AAQ-II

Below you will find a list of statements. Please rate how true each statement is for you by circling a number next to it. Use the scale below to make your choice.

1	2	3	4	5	6	7
never true	very seldom true	seldom true	sometimes true	frequently true	almost always true	always true

1.	My painful experiences and memories make it difficult for me to live a life that I would value.	1	2	3	4	5	6	7
2.	I'm afraid of my feelings.	1	2	3	4	5	6	7
3.	I worry about not being able to control my worries and feelings.	1	2	3	4	5	6	7
4.	My painful memories prevent me from having a fulfilling life.	1	2	3	4	5	6	7
5.	Emotions cause problems in my life.	1	2	3	4	5	6	7
6.	It seems like most people are handling their lives better than I am.	1	2	3	4	5	6	7
7.	Worries get in the way of my success.	1	2	3	4	5	6	7

Permission to print granted by Frank W. Bond

You can also complete the AAQ-OC scale[9] to determine where you are with your obsessions and compulsions. Please read the instructions carefully. You can complete this scale again when you have worked through the workbook.

AAQ-OC

We are interested in your experiences with unwanted intrusive thoughts, ideas, impulses, doubts, images, and feelings that something is "not just right". These experiences may be bizarre, senseless, and unpleasant; they may seem inconsistent with who you are (your personality) and how you see yourself. These experiences may also seem to occur against your will; you may try hard to ignore them, but they keep coming back. Sometimes people feel the need to do something (a behavior or mental action) to try to control or remove these types of unwanted thoughts, images, or doubts in order to feel more comfortable.

The following are some examples of unwanted intrusive thoughts:
- The thought that you might have become contaminated after touching something.
- Doubts about whether or not you locked the door or turned off an appliance when you left home.
- Thoughts or urges to engage in behaviors (related to sex, immorality, or violence) that are against your morals or religious beliefs (e.g., pushing a stranger in front of oncoming traffic; a blasphemous thought).
- Thoughts or feelings that something isn't "just right" (e.g., need for symmetry).

Please note we are NOT referring to daydreams or pleasant fantasies. We are also NOT asking about depressive thoughts (e.g., "I'm worthless") or general worries about everyday matters such as money, school/work, or family issues.

Below you will find a list of statements asking about your experiences with unwanted intrusive thoughts. Please rate how true each statement is for you by selecting a number using the scale below.

1	2	3	4	5	6	7
never true	very seldom true	seldom true	sometimes true	frequently true	almost always true	always true

1. My intrusive thoughts determine the actions that I take.   1 2 3 4 5 6 7
2. I try hard to avoid having intrusive thoughts.   1 2 3 4 5 6 7
3. Intrusive thoughts get in the way of my success.   1 2 3 4 5 6 7
4. It seems like other people are handling their unwanted intrusive thoughts better than I am.   1 2 3 4 5 6 7
5. I need to control my intrusive thoughts in order to handle my life well.   1 2 3 4 5 6 7
6. I stop taking care of my responsibilities when I have intrusive thoughts.   1 2 3 4 5 6 7
7. If an unpleasant intrusive thought comes into my head, I try to get rid of it.   1 2 3 4 5 6 7
8. Intrusive thoughts cause problems in my life.   1 2 3 4 5 6 7
9. I'm afraid of my intrusive thoughts.   1 2 3 4 5 6 7
10. My intrusive thoughts prevent me from leading a fulfilling life.   1 2 3 4 5 6 7
11. I can't stand having intrusive thoughts.   1 2 3 4 5 6 7
12. I worry about not being able to control my intrusive thoughts.   1 2 3 4 5 6 7
13. I try hard to control the physical reactions that I experience in my body when I am having intrusive thoughts (e.g., heart racing, sweating).   1 2 3 4 5 6 7

Permission to print granted by Ryan Jane Jacoby

2

Doing What Matters Most to You

You must want to fly so much that you are willing to give up being a caterpillar.

—*Trina Paulus*

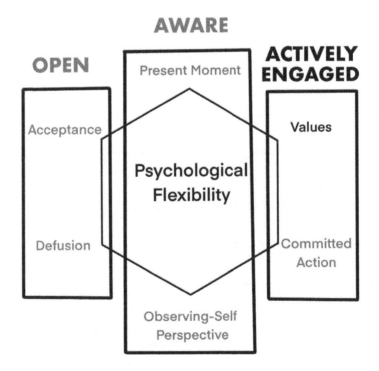

What Do You Want Your Life to Be About?

A caterpillar named Yellow was wondering what to do with her life when she noticed a gray-haired caterpillar hanging upside down on a nearby branch. He seemed to be caught in some kind of hairy stuff. She asked him if she could help as he seemed to be in trouble.

He answered, "No, my dear, I have to do this to become a butterfly." When Yellow heard the word *butterfly*, **her whole insides leapt.** She wanted to know more about what the word *butterfly* meant.

The gray-haired caterpillar said, "It's what you are meant to become. It flies with beautiful wings and joins the earth to heaven. It drinks nectar from the flowers and carries the seeds of love from one flower to another."

Yellow was skeptical. "It can't be true. How can I believe there's a butterfly inside you or me when all I see is a fuzzy worm? How does one become a butterfly?" she asked pensively.

"**You must want to fly so much you are willing to give up being a caterpillar,**" he answered. **Yellow decided to risk becoming a butterfly.** For courage, she hung right beside the other cocoon and began to spin her own."[1]

> What are you willing to give up so you can become what you wish to be? It takes courage to enter the darkness in order to be transformed and reach your potential despite the daily challenges you face.

What Makes Your Whole Insides Leap?

I'd guess that you care about spirituality and morality because OCD would not be targeting those values if you didn't.

> "What causes my whole insides to leap?"

Ponder this question throughout this chapter and workbook. What matters most in your life and how you go about living according to it will keep you going even when you face difficulty.

It has been said that we are what we do. I'd like to add:

> We are what we **do**, and what we **do** is, hopefully,
> what we **value and care about most**.

The following exercise can help you see your life with a broader vision of what matters most.

Exercise 1. Attending Your Own Funeral[2]

This exercise may seem morbid, but it's never too early or late to recognize what you want your life to be about despite what the anxious mind is telling you. This exercise can help if you've been distracted by certain activities, such as trying to control internal events (e.g., your thoughts and feelings).

I invite you to imagine what the epitaph on your tombstone will say. Picture your loved ones talking about you and trying to decide what to inscribe. What would they write based on the way you lived your life?

What would you like your loved ones to say to celebrate your life when you pass on?

Consider the following questions as you write your epitaph:

- Am I trying to live a meaningful life every day?
- Do my loved ones know what and who matters most to me?
- Does what I do every day align with what I want my life to stand for?

Now, write your epitaph:

Once you've written your epitaph, read it daily. Notice how it changes your outlook and what you do every day. Are you spending your time and energy on what you want your life to be about?

Clarifying What Matters Most to You

Matt's Story

Matt once said, "No one and nothing matters as much as the love I have for my family and friends and living honestly. I do my best, but I feel like OCD has taken it all."

Do you ever feel like Matt? Are there values you've forgotten about or neglected to live up to because of anxiety and OCD?

What Values Are and What They Are Not

Values are the principles that guide and motivate you every day. They help you keep going even during difficult times. A helpful indication that you've chosen your true values (internal or external voices aside) is that they allow you to be open to new things, willing to experience discomfort, and focused on the present moment.

For example, if OCD wasn't getting in the way of his values, Matt would regularly spend time with his loved ones. He'd strive to be the type of person he wants to be without getting stuck wondering whether he's loving or honest enough, just to appease his anxious mind.

His epitaph could say, "Matt was a loving and honorable man." His loved ones would share stories about how they saw him living according to what he valued. His values were constant and lasting until the day he died.

At times, you may believe that your safety behaviors (compulsions) are in the service of your values. Be clear that whatever actions you take, if you are doing them to find relief from anxiety, uncertainty, guilt, shame, or other stressful feelings or thoughts, you are most likely stuck in the OCD cycle. Values are not the thoughts, feelings, or actions you use to find relief from discomfort.

For example, if Matt spends *excessive* hours worrying about and looking over his business files to ensure he is paying his taxes 100 percent honestly, he may believe he's engaging in these behaviors (compulsions) because he values honesty. He may not realize that whatever the behavior he engages in, if it is to find relief from difficult or unwanted internal experiences (e.g., thoughts, memories, feelings, and sensations), he is most likely stuck in the scrupulosity trap (OCD cycle) and actually moving away from what he values.

This workbook will provide you with the skills you need to see your internal experiences from a different perspective so you can truly live according to your values and not the anxious mind.

Exercise 2. Recognizing Your Values[3]

Take time to thoughtfully answer the questions below. Your answers don't need to be what you think you "should" or "ought to" say because someone else, society, or your anxious mind says so. Maintain an open attitude as you discover what makes your whole insides leap.

Questions to ponder:

- If money, time, or anything else were not a challenge to you achieving something meaningful in the world, what would you be doing? Think about what actions others might see you doing as you live according to your values.

- What would the purpose of this effort be?

- Who would you invite to participate in this achievement?

- As you think about the people you'd like to help you, what characteristics and qualities do you admire in those people?

- If scrupulosity OCD were not an issue, what personal characteristics would you develop and/or strengthen? How could these qualities help you live more meaningfully?

- What life domains (e.g., relationships, education/work, personal growth/health, spirituality, recreation/leisure) are important to you, and what would you be doing in each area that shows you care?

- If a loved one could see you from afar, could they tell by your actions that you were living a meaningful life in the life domains that matter most to you? For instance, if you valued learning, would your loved ones see you reading or attending a class? If relationships mattered to you, how would you spend time with your loved ones?

As you become more focused on who and what matters most to you, you will find that life has more to offer and that you don't have to listen to the anxious mind.

Exercise 3. Choosing Your Top Ten Values
(What You Want Your Life to Be About)

Look at the list below and determine which values you are already living and which you wish to live that bring you joy. This list is not complete. If the values you espouse are not listed, please add them in the space provided.

Acceptance	Competition	Equanimity	Humor
Adventure	Confidence	Excitement	Humility
Advocacy	Connection	Fitness	Independence
Authenticity	Cooperation	Flexibility	Integrity
Boldness	Creativity	Forgiveness	Intimacy
Caring	Curiosity	Freedom	Justice
Challenge	Dependability	Fun	Kindness
Change	Determination	Generosity	Knowledge
Charity	Diligence	Genuineness	Leadership
Commitment	Empathy	Gratitude	Learning
Communication	Encouragement	Hard work	Love
Compassion	Endurance	Honesty	Loyalty
Competence	Equality	Hope	Morality

Nature	Privacy	Security	Spirituality
Openness	Punctuality	Self-discipline	Stability
Optimism	Respect	Self-development	Support
Organization	Responsibility	Sense of humor	Traditions
Patience	Romance	Service	Trustworthiness
Perseverance	Savoring moments	Simplicity	Wisdom

List Any Additional Values Here:

My Top Ten Values

1.	6.
2.	7.
3.	8.
4.	9.
5.	10.

Once you've listed your top ten values, narrow it down to your top five. You may want to review the previous questions or answer these additional questions to help you decide.

- If all of a sudden you found yourself in a distant galaxy, how would you live your life? Would you do what matters most to you to keep living meaningfully?

- Would your passions and the quality of actions you took every day bring you joy despite being far away from home?

> Your top five values can be what keep you going during difficult times.

My Top Five Values

1.	
2.	
3.	
4.	
5.	

Focus on the Process

Please remember that the process is **not** about goals or milestones. A former client talking about the process and living his values instead of just focusing on goals once said, "Yeah, the question is, 'Do I just want to climb Mount Everest or enjoy climbing?'" He realized he didn't need to rush the process.

The process is about making small changes, improving, and, most importantly, enjoying the journey as you live your values. Don't compare yourself to others. Your journey is yours alone. Don't confuse effort to improve with being consumed with obsessions and compulsions to the point of exhaustion.

Exercise 4. Living Your Values Is an Ongoing Choice[4]

Once you've come up with your top five values (remember, there is no rush to get through this chapter or section), notice how they play a role in what you do and in the decisions you make day to day.

As you go about life engaging in what matters most, notice your answers to the questions in the graphic below. As you continue to read this workbook and life begins to open up, you will no longer be ruled by your anxious mind. You'll discover the freedom to keep moving toward your values even when discomfort is present. You'll also recognize that you can be imperfectly good and enjoy your faith and other values!

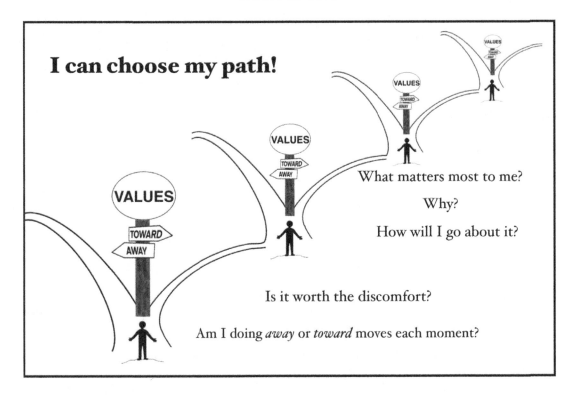

One last question to help you choose your values:

When I face adversity, why is the pain worth having?

Come back to this chapter as often as you need to throughout your reading.

What we care about most counts only when we act on it!

3

Understanding the Mind

Take on risks and ride the journey called life without regrets.
—D. K. Olukoya

Life's Journey

A few years ago, my family went on vacation to Costa Rica, where we went white-water rafting. The night before our rafting trip, I looked at the promotional brochure. It said the river rating classification was four to five. None of us knew what that meant as we had never been white-water rafting before. We were about to find out.

Right before we took off, the guide reminded us that once we were on the river, there was no turning back because the area was surrounded by dense tropical forest. I had a chance to change my mind, but I didn't. I didn't want to miss out on enjoying the river. I was in for the ride of my life!

When we hit the rapids, I kept thinking I should have stayed behind. I was so terrified that, most of the time, I clung to the raft instead of helping paddle. At times, our guide's commands were insufficient as we tried to avoid strong currents and boulders. When we came to a point called El Chorro ("the faucet" in Spanish), even with everyone paddling and doing their best, we simply couldn't make it and our raft capsized.

Perhaps it was because I wasn't doing my part, but two of my sons, the guide, and I were thrown out and went under. I think the others surfaced right away, but I wasn't sure if I was ever going to come up. I thought I was going to drown as the current pulled me under. I was glad I remembered these instructions: "If you fall into the water, don't let go of the paddle no matter what." Eventually, I was able to get to a pool of calm water, where I waited to be rescued.

As I began to write this workbook, I thought of my rafting experience and my clients who struggle with fears related to their scrupulosity OCD. Many of them report, "It is as if I'm drowning on dry land." So they fight for their lives and do whatever they can to escape the turbulent waters within. Their frightful experiences seem endless.

What Does Scrupulosity OCD Feel Like for You?

If you don't relate to the drowning metaphor, what does scrupulosity OCD feel like for you? What is it like when you have the urge to live your faith and other values perfectly?

In the space below, write what it feels like. If you are willing, draw it. Abstract art, stick figures, or anything you can think of to externalize what scrupulosity OCD feels like for you is fine. I've noticed that when clients draw what it feels like for them, they begin to change their relationship with it.

Please be patient with whatever feelings arise related to your experiences with scrupulosity OCD. You're going to learn how to respond to them. For now, just take a moment to notice your thoughts and emotions after drawing and writing about your religious and moral anxiety.

You can also give your scrupulosity OCD a name. I'll be referring to it as "the scrupulous mind" throughout the workbook. Once you name it, it'll be easier for you to treat it as a separate entity. Naming the OCD mind can enhance your flexibility toward it. Some people use names, such as Bob or Carlota. Call it anything. Just be gentle with it. After all, your mind means well.

My scrupulosity OCD mind's name is: _____

Note how you feel once you've named it:

Adversity Is Part of the Journey

> *I do not believe that sheer suffering teaches. If suffering alone taught, all the world would be wise, since everyone suffers. To suffering must be added mourning, understanding, patience, love, openness, and the willingness to remain vulnerable.*
>
> —Anne Morrow Lindbergh[1]

As we travel through the turbulent waters of life, the different types of challenges we encounter can help us mature emotionally. Indeed, adversity is part of life, and being free of it all before finding joy in life is a futile proposition of the scrupulous mind.

There Is Opposition in All Things

Evan's Story

Evan believed he had to sacrifice not only his happiness but everything he cared about to serve everyone around him. He often beat himself up for not being a good enough son, relative, friend, neighbor, worker, etc. Whenever he was having a good time with his friends, he'd feel guilty and think, "I don't deserve this happiness." And he would obsess about what he "should" be doing to serve others instead of enjoying time with his friends.

What Evan didn't realize was that his struggles wouldn't exist if he didn't value service and connection with others. Because he valued these things, he experienced emotional pain whenever he felt like he wasn't doing enough to be kind and serve others. But just because he experienced pain, it didn't mean he had to let go of the things he cared about most.

Many say, "If I just stop believing or abandon certain values, maybe the pain will go away." They later discover that abandoning their morals, values, and beliefs is not the answer.

If you have OCD, avoidance may not be the best solution, even though the mind may propose that as the only option.

> Are the struggles you are experiencing related to what's most important to you?

You may value your morals and/or religious beliefs but feel you are not living in accordance with them. No matter how much you try to do so, guilt, anxiety, and doubts about yourself and your intentions persist. Clearly, there is opposition in all things. You would not be experiencing your current challenges regarding your morals and/or religion if you did not care about your morals or religion. The truth is, "You hurt where you care."[2]

> You don't have to wait for your trials to be gone to start living life.
> You don't need to change what you care about most.
> Instead, you can change how you see your struggles.

Ponder and answers these questions:

- What have I postponed or stopped doing because of my emotional, physical, or mental challenges?

- How long has it been since I've joined in any of these activities?

- If my challenges were absent, what would I be doing with my life?

- What do I want my life to be about despite the uncertainty I often experience?

- Have there been any losses in my relationships, education/work, personal growth/health, spirituality, recreation/leisure because I've been trying to live my faith and other values perfectly?

> Life is an adventure that includes ups and downs.
> While we all experience pain of one kind or another,
> how we respond to that pain makes a big difference in our suffering.

Ryan's Story

As a child, Ryan began exhibiting symptoms of OCD with constant worries about contamination. When he was a teenager, he enjoyed a "worldly" path before finding his faith. One day, after he'd found his faith, however, a friend made a comment that brought up certain memories from his youth. Sexual images popped into his mind. He tried to replace them with wholesome images, but he couldn't get rid of the unwanted images and consequently felt immoral and unworthy of God's blessings.

When the environment (trigger) activated recollections of his past, Ryan thought he could "control" his internal experiences (e.g., thoughts, memories, judgments, emotions, sensations, and urges) by replacing the awful images with wholesome thoughts. "I'll memorize a scripture verse so I won't have these images," he'd say. "If I try harder, I can stop them!" But the images persisted, and shame often took over when he couldn't "control" them.

The Mind as the "Protector"

The amazing brain, with its billions of neurons and trillions of connections and cells, is part of who we are, but *we are not our brain*, just like we are not our stomach or the other parts of our bodies. They are part of us, but we are not them.

The mind is the result of what occurs in the brain all day long. Thoughts, emotions, urges, memories, and sensations are the internal, private events that occur through the mind. The mind produces internal experiences all day long and offers us advice when it perceives something is wrong. We could say the mind is an adviser and protector designed to help us survive the world around us.

When we feel anxious, guilty, or inadequate, our mind automatically gets ready to protect us. Our instinct is to listen to it even when there is no apparent physical danger. ("Don't pray. Providence will not accept your prayers if you don't stay focused!")

Thoughts such as "I'm not worthy." "I'd better avoid that situation." "I'm not good enough." "I may be responsible for others' suffering!" "I'm living a privileged life. Shame on me!" can trigger you to beat yourself up or avoid life because doing so seems like the safe thing to do.

Even though you may be worthy, good enough, and doing your best to live your values (e.g., caring and serving), the scrupulous mind may insist on giving you unhelpful advice. The question is, does listening to it allow you to do what matters most to you and bring you peace and joy?

The human mind is an incredible gift, but we must learn to recognize when it offers unhelpful advice ("You need to serve *everyone* you meet today!") and goes overboard to protect us!

A Double-Edged Sword

Humankind's unique ability to process thoughts and make connections to past or future events differentiates us from every other living species. Despite continued experiments and efforts to get certain species to "think" like we do, no other species can do so because they lack this ability and the complexity of our language.

However, the ability to make all these connections between past and future events can be a double-edged sword.

On one hand, because of this ability, we can go to space, create artificial intelligence, invent lifesaving equipment, and accomplish many other amazing things. Yet, because we can think and communicate in this way, we can also become depressed, anxious, and even self-destructive.

Because of this, we need to be able to recognize that our well-meaning, marvelous mind does not always provide advice that helps us live our values, especially if OCD is in the middle of it all.

Pain × Resistance = Suffering

We all experience pain in various forms. However, when we resist or push down our emotional pain (e.g., unpleasant thoughts and feelings), we inadvertently multiply that pain.

Have you noticed what happens when you try to push a beach ball underwater? As much as you want it to stay under, it always comes back up—and it might even hit you in the face!

So it is when we try to suppress uncomfortable thoughts and feelings. Though battling with them appears to make sense, it actually exacerbates the issue. When we focus on avoiding or preventing pain, we are thinking about the pain, and we therefore make it last longer. And as we fight it, we can miss out on enjoying life.

Can You Toss Your Thoughts and Feelings Away?

In the external world, you can replace or toss away what is not useful. When your favorite pair of shoes wears out, you simply buy a new pair and toss out the old ones.

You can't toss your thoughts, feelings, and other internal events like you would an old pair of shoes, though your mind might tell you that you can. Is that advice working for you?

Can You Delete Them?

Complete the Following Sentences:

Humpty Dumpty _____

Jack and Jill _____

When was the last time you thought about these rhymes? If you have children in your life, it may have been recently, but for some of you, it may be since you were a kid. Why haven't you forgotten those childhood rhymes?

You may have thoughts and images you wish you could delete from your memory. We all do. Even if you try to get rid of them a thousand times, they keep coming back. It is nearly impossible to purposely delete facts from our minds as we delete something on our electronic devices. If you don't like someone's comments on your social media feed, you just unfollow them or delete their name. Done!

Wouldn't life be paradise if we could rid ourselves of painful thoughts and feelings like we delete obnoxious individuals from our social media feeds?

When you experience unpleasant thoughts, you may try to relieve the associated stress by avoiding them and engaging in strategies like suppression and ignoring. But no matter how much you try, it doesn't work. The thoughts just keep recurring.

> Your mind provides you with solutions that work well with external events, but similar solutions are not effective when it comes to internal experiences.

Exercise 1. Our Lives Are Intertwined with Anything and Everything

Think about a distressing word or thought you wish you could delete from your memory. Write it below, then write a "replacement" by using a neutral or positive word or thought.

Unwanted thought/word/image: _____

Replacement thought/word/image: _____

The next time this unpleasant word shows up, quickly replace it with your chosen neutral or positive word. Do it often and notice what happens when you keep adding a "replacement." Then write down what you've learned below.

Research[3] shows that when we try to replace a word with another word, we actually create a new relationship between the two words or the objects those words describe. If we replace the second with a third, fourth, fifth, and so on, we have multiplied the relationship instead of deleting it!

We simply cannot delete our thoughts, feelings, or other internal experiences from our minds. We are continually creating relationships between things. That's just the way our minds operate because we have language, the ability to communicate, remember, and relate anything to everything.

Maybe you already know that what you've been doing does not work. If you are new to this concept, however, you'll soon learn that replacing or trying to delete something from your mind simply does not work.

> The good news is that you can learn you don't have to be bound by the rules your mind is trying to impose upon you.
> You can become flexible with what your mind tells you.

Awareness Questions

Take your time answering the following questions:

- When I experience painful thoughts and feelings, have I noticed what my mind advises me to do, and do I act on it to find relief?

- Does my mind create rules and expectations for how things "should" be, like "I'm not supposed to have these thoughts," "I shouldn't have had that thought about someone," or simply "This is bad!"? What are the rules my mind comes up with?

- What feelings and physical sensations do I feel, and what do I normally do about them?

- What happens when I wish for something other than what's happening in the moment? Is my emotional pain magnified?

- Is it possible that these unpleasant thoughts, feelings, and other internal experiences are not the real problem?

> The relationship we have with painful internal experiences and the belief that we are not supposed to have them is the real challenge.

The Man in a Hole[4]

There once lived a man who was blindfolded and sent into a large field. He was given a bag with a tool, just in case he needed it. He went about life as best he could, but occasionally, he would fall into small and medium holes. Luckily, he always managed to get out.

One day, he fell into a large hole. He blamed not only those who'd put him there but also himself. He obsessed and lamented about what he could have done to avoid his situation. "What could I have done to avoid falling into this large hole?" he wondered again and again. But no matter how many times he mentally reviewed his actions, the fact remained that he was in the hole.

Then he remembered the bag he had been given. He opened it, found a shovel inside, and decided to dig himself out. But he blindly began to shovel himself deeper into the hole. The more he dug, the deeper he got. He became desperate. It was all he could do, and sometimes he thought he might be digging the wrong way, so he tried big shovelfuls. At other times he tried small shovelfuls. But no matter what he did, he found himself stuck in the hole. Day in and day out, he dug and dug and dug.

Those who struggle with OCD often feel like this man; they feel like their compulsions are necessary in order to feel at peace the rest of the day.

Let's explore what happens when you get stuck trying to get out of the scrupulosity trap by "digging" your way out (giving in to private or public compulsions).

Exercise 2. The Resourceful Mind and Unhelpful Shovels

No human being is free of challenges, and our resourceful mind is always ready to advise us on how to avoid these challenges and feel better. The mind can lead you to believe some of your behaviors are helpful when at times they may actually be digging you deeper into the scrupulosity trap.

Your thoughts, emotions, and sensations can become so distressing that the urge to "pick up a shovel" becomes irresistible. It often seems like the coping strategies you are using are providing you with long-term results. The short-term relief they provide may motivate you to keep doing those behaviors, which unintentionally become compulsions.

Try using the acronym DOTS[5] to help you notice when you are using strategies that may seem harmless but which, if you are doing them with the sole purpose of escaping or fighting your painful thoughts, feelings, physical sensations, and other internal events, may be getting you stuck in the scrupulosity trap.

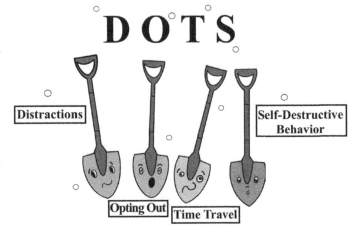

Distractions

Can distractions *truly* help you forget your worries (e.g., watching TV or engaging in social media to forget about possibly offending a friend)? Of course, they can help you temporarily, but in using distractions to help you forget about your worries, you are actually resisting those worries and putting them off, which can result in more suffering.

- What distractions do you default to in order to resist or push away your thoughts and feelings? Notice, then jot down anything you might use as distractions. Remember, they appear harmless, but in the long run, they only reinforce the scrupulosity trap.

Opting Out

How often do you avoid or opt out of situations because they cause anxiety, uncertainty, or other unpleasant emotions? What's the difference between distractions and avoidance anyway?

Let's discuss avoidance in more detail.

Tracy's Story

Before scrupulosity OCD showed up in Tracy's life, she enjoyed going to religious services, but she eventually stopped attending to avoid feelings of anxiety and feeling unworthy of God's love. Staying away from her spiritual activities seemed to solve the problem. However, she often yearned for connection with God and her friends.

Steve Hayes and other ACT researchers have found that, like Tracy, individuals who try to avoid painful emotions (e.g., anxiety) exhibit two types of pain: the *pain of presence* and the *pain of absence*.[6]

Pain of Presence

The "pain of presence" refers to the pain associated with being in situations you perceive as anxiety-producing. When anxiety or other harrowing feelings mount, you avoid them, like Tracy did. Tracy chose to stay away from religious activities because of the anxiety and guilt she experienced. Yet, despite her avoidance, her anxiety and guilt were still present.

Pain of Absence

The "pain of absence" refers to the pain that comes from the activities and people you're missing out on because of your unwillingness to experience difficult emotions. The problem is that when Tracy stayed away from the things causing her unpleasant feelings, she paradoxically experienced the pain of absence. Sadly, because of her anxiety related to scrupulosity OCD, she was missing out on the things that mattered most to her—her relationships with the Almighty and her fellow worshipers.

Avoidance brings pain not only because you are missing out on the life you want to live but also because it doesn't fix things. The unwanted feelings and thoughts don't go away. Avoidance does not change the pain or get rid of it. Avoidance can also cause long-term negative consequences, such as depression and loneliness.

- When have you experienced the pain of absence?

- When have you experienced the pain of presence?

- What might you be missing out on because of avoidance?

- Is your avoidance getting in the way of you living your values—the things that matter most?

Time Travel

You don't need a transporter, like the *Star Trek* crew, to get from one place to another. You don't need a time machine, like Doc and Marty McFly's DeLorean, to move backward or forward in time. Your mind is your very own time machine;

in less than a microsecond, it can take you to the past or future. And the mind often takes us to the past or future in an attempt to "make things better."

- Where does your "time machine" like to take you?

- How often do you find yourself reviewing every detail of a recent or distant past event you wish had turned out differently?

- How often do you anticipate with anxiety a future event to the point you feel ill?

- When has time-traveling been effective for you?

It has been said, "Learn from the past, prepare for the future, and live in the present." In this workbook, you'll be learning skills to help you live in the present.

Self-Destructive Behavior

Sometimes the scrupulous mind will tell you that certain activities, such as playing video games late into the night, are helpful. Playing video games can be fun, but it can be harmful if you start missing out on life.

Anything you do that is **not** helping you live purposefully and joyfully can become harmful. Are you oversleeping, not sleeping enough, or over- or undereating? Are you overusing TV and social media? You might be using these activities to distract yourself, to opt out, or as self-destructive behavior. Are these behaviors hurting your studies, work, and relationships and therefore your emotional and mental well-being?

What other strategies are you using to find relief from your internal experiences?

A behavior that appears to be a great thing in the moment may actually be getting in the way of healthy emotional functioning.

Exercise 3. Tallying Unhelpful Strategies

At any given time, you can notice when your mind is telling you to use **DOTS** or other coping tools that don't provide long-term results. I invite you to keep a tally on your smartphone throughout the day to see if you are using your mind's favorite tools to help you cope temporarily.

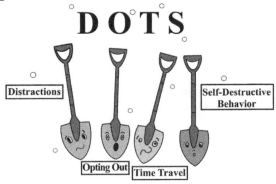

- **D**istractions:
- **O**pting out:
- **T**ime travel:
- **S**elf-destructive behavior:

- Other behaviors:

4
Recognizing Your Internal Experiences

Linda's Story

When Linda's therapist asked what she hoped to get out of treatment, she responded, "I just want you to teach me skills so I can control my thoughts and my feelings. I need to feel righteous all the time." Soon enough, Linda learned she could respond to internal experiences and *change her relationship with them* instead of trying to control them.

Your Response to External and Internal Experiences

Your body is constantly receiving signals (e.g., sounds and words that remind you of past experiences) from the environment, even if you don't want it to. If you get triggered, you may frantically try to get rid of the memories, thoughts, and feelings those signals evoke in that moment. What happens when you do so? Have you been successful at eliminating your painful thoughts, feelings, and other internal events?

Let's see what a natural event like rain can teach you about responding to your internal experiences.

Rain, Rain, Go Away!

Suppose you've planned a picnic. You are excited about it, but since the weather can be unpredictable, you have a plan B. The day of the picnic looks clear, but three hours before the party, rain clouds start to form. You could sing "Rain, rain, go away; come

again another day," but you know you cannot control the rain. You could pray for it to go away, but others may be praying for rain. It rains, and though you are disappointed that the weather did not cooperate, you accept the fact that it's raining and simply go to plan B.

You get to choose how to respond to the rain and how to adjust to something you cannot control. You would not try to fight **a natural event** like rain.

> Likewise, it is important to recognize that
> our internal experiences are like rain–
> they're **natural events**.
> They are part of everyday life.
> Even though the scrupulous mind tells you
> that you can fight and control them, you can't.

There is a way to respond to your internal events, and it's not the way the scrupulous mind thinks you should.

Let's take time to review and learn more about our internal experiences.

Thoughts

The words you hear are speech, the words you read are text, and the words that come from your mind are thoughts.[1] Thoughts often consist of opinions, evaluations, or assumptions related to how you feel at any given moment.

The question is, do you believe every word you hear and read? Most likely not. So do you need to believe every word (i.e., thought) your mind provides? Thoughts are part of your inside world. They are natural, internal, private events, and do you need to believe every word your mind says? Perhaps not.

Your values are your guiding influence. But should you find yourself unable to control your thoughts, you may believe you have failed God and others or that God has failed you. You may think there's something wrong with you. ("I'm bad because a swear word showed up when I was thinking of God.") The scrupulous mind may insist you are your thoughts. But, remember, you are not your brain; therefore, you are also not your mind or thoughts. And yes, they are part of your human experience.

Thoughts Have No Intrinsic Meaning

What internal experiences arise as you read the following words?

¿Hize trampa en mi reporte de impuestos?

Huh?

These words won't trigger you unless you know Spanish, the scrupulous mind is targeting your value of honesty, and you tend to get stuck with the content or meaning of your thoughts.

Did I cheat on my tax return?

Now, you may have gotten stuck with those words. Your mind's tendency to give meaning to and find relationships with certain events (real or perceived) happens quickly.

正直

If you don't know Chinese, these are just lines. Your mind can't create a relationship with them. What happens when you know these lines mean "integrity"?

Notice how quickly your mind comes up with thoughts or words to give *integrity* a meaning that could get you stuck.

The point is that thoughts are just words; they have only the meaning you attribute to them. You may categorize your thoughts as "bad" because of the relationship you have with them. We are able to attach meaning to anything and everything because of our experiences and our capacity for language, but these connections are not always helpful.

What thoughts tend to get you stuck because of the meaning your mind assigns them? For example, if someone says the word *taxes*, your anxious mind may fixate on the time you *thought* you cheated on your taxes. You probably didn't, but even just hearing the word creates intense anxiety, doubt, and guilt. You get caught up in the *meaning* your mind has linked to that word.

Write the words that get you stuck. Remember, you get stuck with them because of the relationships your mind has created.

Memories

Imagine a universe in which your feelings, thoughts, and memories are not your enemy. They are your history brought into the current context, and your own history is not your enemy.

—*Steven C. Hayes*[2]

Sophia's Story

Sophia was visiting her sister and fifteen-year-old niece. When her niece came back from babysitting, she told Sophia the child she had been watching had dumped his toys in the living room and tripped over them.

Hearing her niece's story triggered Sophia's memory of a similar experience she'd had when she was fourteen years old. She had forgotten about the incident, but the more she thought about it, the more anxious she became. She hadn't ever told the family about the incident. "Did I mean to hide it? Was the child brain-damaged? Is that why he sat so quietly in the corner of the room?" These incessant thoughts related to the memory tormented her. She believed it was her duty to find the family and tell them about it, even though the family had moved to another state.

> Note: Please make sure you don't misunderstand this conversation. In this workbook, I'm referring to events your OCD magnifies and torments you with because of uncertainty. I'm not referring to incidents that were traumatic in nature. Trauma is a different topic, and if you've experienced trauma and also struggle with OCD, please make sure you see a mental health provider to help you through this serious challenge.

Is Your Scrupulosity OCD Nagging You?

You may have memories that make you feel uncertain. If those memories relate to the values the scrupulous mind is currently targeting, you may feel tormented by incessant doubt and guilt.

Whatever your behaviors were in the past, they may have been facts at the time, but they are memories now (like a movie or video clip in your head). You may have apologized, repented, and done whatever else was needed to move on, yet the memories linger. You may be stuck with them and believe, "The memories and feelings must be an indication that I didn't truly repent." You may have the urge to push them away from your awareness or start ruminating about whether you really did something wrong, confessed every detail, or repented thoroughly.

Trying to make sense of a memory because the scrupulous mind insists you should does not change what already happened or what you perceived happened. The event is no longer a fact; it's a memory. You do the best you can to find peace when you make mistakes or misbehave. However, sometimes the scrupulous mind may not allow you to move on. It may insist you haven't done enough, and when you listen to it, you can become stuck in the scrupulosity trap.

Your mind may also create additional relationships with words, objects, images, and events that multiply every time you go back in time. You may even be inadvertently creating false memories.

The Time Machine

When the mind brings up thoughts about the past (or the future), you may feel like you are right there, living in that moment. You may forget you are here right now as you become consumed in thoughts, such as:

- If I had genuinely repented, this would not bother me anymore.
- If I had walked away, these images would not be here.
- My future spouse will think I am despicable!

A memory or worry about the past cannot be *solved* because it is an internal, natural event. It was once a fact, but now, all you have is the "video clip." And while the past is in the past, the thought about the past can feel overwhelming in the present!

Exercise 1. Noticing Relationship Links

As mentioned earlier, whether you have a pleasant or unpleasant thought, that thought will lead to another thought and another. Your amazing language machine—the mind—allows you to problem-solve and link "anything to anything at the speed of thought."[3]

Sit in a quiet place for three to five minutes. Read these instructions and then proceed to notice when your mind starts producing thoughts. Watch out! They come fast! At one point, you may get stuck with a difficult thought, evaluation, or memory, and you may even forget you're in the middle of this exercise. That's okay. Once you are no longer stuck, continue noticing.

As you become aware of the links between your thoughts, continue to observe them as an unbiased onlooker. The mind may want you to ruminate about what comes up. As soon as you become aware that you are ruminating, gently go back to noticing.

It is fascinating how quickly the mind works and to realize how one random thought can lead to another and eventually to a memory or thought that gets you stuck.

Write about what you've just learned by noticing how quickly the links are formed.

Take a few minutes throughout your day to notice how quickly your mind links one internal event to another.

Sometimes you may want to stay with a thought or memory that's pleasant. If you have time to enjoy that memory, by all means, enjoy it!

Evaluations

Fred's Story

Fred was constantly evaluating his behavior around others. The more he wanted to be humble, the more self-critical he became. "I'm such an idiot. When I got mad at my brother, all I could think of was that I'm better than he is." "I need to be humble around others."

You may be familiar with judgmental thoughts like these. The problem is that, sometimes, when the mind tells us these kinds of things, we listen too attentively.

Exercise 2. The Judgmental Mind

- I'm not worthy of love.
- I'm bad.
- I'm not trying hard enough.

When you are not able to live according to your values and beliefs, are you afraid God and others will judge you? Is it possible your mind is just trying to help you and is getting ahead of the game? "If I beat myself up before anyone else does, it won't be as painful." What has your experience been?

List some of the judgmental thoughts you have about yourself that you've noticed lately. Do you believe them, and what happens when you do?

Some claim self-criticism helps them work harder and improves their performance. But does self-criticism help you become more confident and empowered? Research indicates otherwise.[4]

It has been said,

"The brain takes the shape of whatever the mind rests upon."[5]

Self-criticism may work temporarily, but the longer you occupy yourself with it, the more hopeless and depressed you will feel. We'll address this in more detail in a future chapter.

Whenever you feel uncertain about your worthiness, intentions, or behaviors, your mind will provide advice to help you do something about it because we human beings yearn for coherence. The self-judgments you experience come from a well-meaning mind doing the job it was designed to do.

Awareness Questions

Notice your answers when you're self-critical after a difficult day:

- Do I feel motivated when I am harsh with myself? If so, is that motivation effective in the long run?

- Do I feel optimistic and full of hope when I beat myself up?

- Am I truly able to improve my character and resilience when I criticize myself?

- Is the scrupulous mind getting in the way of me taking chances in life?

Be self-aware but not self-critical.

Feelings

Feelings can't be ignored, no matter how unjust or ungrateful they seem.
—Anne Frank[6]

Kayley's Story

Kayley valued kindness, love, and service. She also believed she should avoid certain emotions. For example, when she did a kind deed and felt joy, she suppressed the joy because she was afraid of becoming prideful. When her roommate "borrowed" her favorite jacket without asking, she suppressed her anger. Eventually, she became depressed.

Feelings Have a Function

As we receive cues (e.g., hearing someone shout "Fire!") from the external world, our mind produces thoughts, emotions, urges, memories, and sensations related to those cues. When we perceive danger, our mind and body help us feel fear so we can protect ourselves from harm. In this case, we can say fear is helpful because without it, our ancestors would not have survived and we would not be here.

You may say, "I get it, but what about sadness?" It serves a purpose too. Imagine your best friend's mother dies. If you were able to get rid of sadness because it was a "bad" feeling, how would you comfort your best friend if you couldn't sympathize with her?

How We Respond to Our Feelings Is What Matters

When someone wrongs us, we may feel angry. Is this wrong? No! But if we get stuck in our emotions and react inappropriately, this can be a problem.

Sometimes the behaviors we choose to express our anger, sadness, anxiety, and even happiness can be damaging. The way we respond (e.g., yelling or hurting someone when we are angry) is what gives some feelings a bad reputation. Feelings in and of themselves are neither good nor bad. It is when we respond to them without awareness that we create difficulties. We all have a choice when it comes to how we respond to our feelings.

Exercise 3. How Am I Responding to My Feelings?

Note how you respond to the feelings listed below. Add any feelings not listed that you experience often. You may want to keep track of your responses for a few days.

Feeling	My Response to This Feeling	How Helpful or Unhelpful Was my Response?	What Did I Learn?
Anxiety			
Uncertainty			
Happiness			

Feeling	My Response to This Feeling	How Helpful or Unhelpful Was my Response?	What Did I Learn?
Rejection			
Despair			
Joy			
Hopelessness			
Stress			
Anger			
Sadness			
Guilt			
Shame			

A variety of feelings will show up throughout the day, and different circumstances can determine how we feel. At times we may be able to control external situations so we can avoid certain feelings, but other times we simply cannot. Though avoidance can be helpful at times (e.g., when we are in real danger), avoidance may not be the best option when it gets in the way of living meaningfully.

The good news is that you can choose what to do with your feelings once they are set in motion. You will learn how to do so in a few pages.

Feelings bring color into your life!

—Former Client

Sensations

Cindy's Story

Cindy woke up experiencing tingling in her arms and a pit in her stomach, and she immediately thought, "Oh no! It's going to be a bad day." She hated these bodily sensations, and the more she tried to ignore them, the more they seemed to be there. When she went to school and her professor gave a pop quiz, her abdominal distress became intolerable. She felt deathly ill because she feared she might inadvertently cheat. Her feelings and sensations seemed to be her guiding influence. If she was free of stress and uncomfortable bodily sensations, it was a "good" day.

What's It Like for You?

It's natural to want to get rid of unpleasant sensations, such as abdominal distress, shortness of breath, trembling, profuse sweating, an accelerated heartbeat, and chest pain. If the thought, "Those sensations are not supposed to be there," shows up, a struggle ensues because we cannot simply will them away (see page 40).

One day, I asked Cindy if there was a time in her life when she felt those sensations while doing something fun, like riding a roller coaster. She smiled and said, "Well, I've never ridden a roller coaster, but I like jumping from cliffs into the ocean." I asked, "So, what did you feel? Did you experience an adrenaline rush?" She smiled and said, "I see what you mean. I guess the sensations I experience when I'm jumping off a cliff are the same as when I'm worrying." I asked, "So what's the difference?" She said, "It's the situation." She viewed her feelings and sensations as "bad" whenever she *thought* she shouldn't have them.

In this workbook, you'll learn how to change your relationship with difficult bodily sensations instead of getting stuck in the scrupulosity trap. For now, give the following exercise a go. It is designed to help you be more aware of how you can "be" with your bodily sensations and not react to them.

Exercise 4. Body Scan

Find a comfortable place to sit or lie down for three to five minutes. Read the instructions several times and then proceed with the exercise. You may want to use the recording app on your smartphone so you can listen to the instructions as often as you'd like.

- Take a deep breath, and as you exhale, make a whooshing sound through your mouth. Repeat twice, noticing how your body feels and what your mind is saying.

- Now, pay attention to how your left foot feels. Notice the pressure of your foot against your shoe or the floor. Scan your toes and notice how they feel. Slowly work up your leg to your hip. Don't rush the practice. Pay attention to any sensations you may not have noticed in those areas of your body.

- Now, slowly scan your right foot, leg, and hip. Acknowledge what you notice by saying something like, **"I'm noticing the sensation of** _____ (e.g., a pain in my right foot)."

- Then slowly scan and note any sensations in your pelvic area, stomach, and chest. Notice if there is any discomfort, itchiness, or soreness in these areas. Acknowledge this by saying, **"I'm noticing the sensation of** _____ (e.g., hunger in my stomach)."

- Continue scanning your body by noticing your back and glutes, then pay attention to your neck, face, and head. What do you notice? Is there a scowl on your face? Is there extra heat in the back of your head or neck? Notice and acknowledge, **"I'm noticing a** _____ (e.g., a grimace on my face)."

- Don't try to change anything, even if you have the urge to do so. The purpose of this practice is for you to learn to regularly scan your body and notice the sensations there. Acknowledge: **"I'm noticing the urge to** _____ (e.g., scratch my nose)." Don't fight it. Just keep scanning and noticing.

Take a few minutes every day to scan your body, perhaps when waking up, while you are waiting in line at the grocery store, or as a break from your daily routine.

Urges

Jared's Story

Jared had the urge to rapidly shake his head whenever a distressing thought or other internal event came to his awareness. "Did I just sin with my thoughts? I've got to shake them off!" The urge to respond to the scrupulous mind was irresistible.

Exercise 5. Urges: Do You Have to Act on an Urge Every Time You Have One?

While urges are part of our internal, private experiences, we can learn to create space between those urges and the behaviors that may follow them. Have you noticed the urges you experience? How quickly do you react to them?

Notice whenever an urge shows up and whether you act on it or do something other than what the mind insists you do. You may want to use the chart below to enhance your learning. Are you responding to an urge with private or public compulsions, and are they effective in the long run?

Trigger	Internal Events I Notice (e.g., Thoughts, Feelings, etc.)	What's the Urge?	Private or Public Compulsion?	How Effective Was the Compulsion?
Thought: "Maybe God is not there after all."	Anxiety	Repent, silently pray for forgiveness	Private	Not effective. I felt guilty two minutes later.

The following metaphor can help increase your awareness.

The Passengers in Your Lifeboat

Imagine you're navigating a boat—the boat of your life—and you've picked up some passengers (e.g., difficult thoughts and feelings) along the way. These passengers appear to have created a revolt. They keep telling you which way to go. When you go to places that appear scary and overwhelming, your passengers seem helpful as they tell you to take an easier route.

As the captain of your lifeboat, you want to choose your own route, but the waters are turbulent and unfamiliar. It may feel like you are blindfolded! When your passengers start sharing their opinions, you must decide between continuing on the path you've chosen or giving in to what the others have chosen for you. Sometimes they are so loud you end up blindly following their advice just to keep them quiet.[7]

These passengers are like bullies because you feel like you have no say in what happens each day. It feels like you are no longer in charge of your life because of the deals you've made with them.

You may have tried to ask the loudest and most intimidating passengers to leave because they keep disrupting your journey, but when you try to ignore them or even argue with them, they get louder.

You're so exhausted you may not realize there are some helpful and friendly passengers (e.g., helpful thoughts and feelings) on board. You can't hear them because you are too busy trying to get rid of the loud, unpleasant ones.

If you spend your time consumed with trying to get rid of painful internal experiences, you may miss out on the part of the journey that's meant to be enjoyed. The fear, anxiety, and uncertainty, among other emotions, can feel overwhelming.

To Act or Be Acted Upon

You can learn to act for yourself instead of being bossed around by those unhelpful passengers. You are the captain of your boat!

You can focus your energy on what you can control—the behaviors that take you closer to what and who matters most in your life.

Renowned poet William Henley's words are fitting here. No matter how bad it seems when the scrupulous mind speaks, take courage. You can take your life back!

Invictus

Out of the night that covers me, black as the pit from pole to pole,
I thank whatever gods may be for my unconquerable soul.

In the fell clutch of circumstance, I have not winced nor cried aloud.
Under the bludgeonings of chance my head is bloody, but unbowed.

Beyond this place of wrath and tears looms but the horror of the shade,
and yet the menace of the years finds, and shall find, me unafraid.

It matters not how strait the gate, how charged with punishments the scroll,
I am the master of my fate: I am the captain of my soul.[8]

Rivers, Rocks, and Boulders

The measure of intelligence is the ability to change.

—*Albert Einstein*[9]

In the photo above, you can see the obvious contrast between the water and boulders. Water is the most flexible, moldable substance on Earth. Whatever its recipient, water will take its shape, like a river finds its way through and around the boulders in a river.

As my family floated through the Naranjo River's strong current, boulders occasionally interrupted its flow, but the river found its way around them. Sometimes the rock walls were too narrow, but the river adjusted there as well, creating an exhilarating adventure for those who love white-water rafting. Unlike that flexible, flowing river, I rigidly held the boat's handles to stay in the boat!

When intrusive thoughts occur and you question your faith and other values, some painful internal events may show up that lead you to become rigid and inflexible. As I was white-knuckling those handles, all I could think about was not being thrown out of the raft, and I wasn't able to enjoy the ride.

Exercise 6. The Mind's Unhelpful Roles

We wouldn't be able to function and survive in the world without our minds. Though we no longer have to protect ourselves from menacing creatures roaming the land, it's still the mind's job to watch out for us. When it perceives "danger," it jumps in to save the day by giving us all kinds of advice. It seems the mind is providing rules, solutions, labels, predictions, and pointless sermons all day long.

Let's take a look at how your mind often influences the behaviors (compulsions) that may temporarily provide comfort and reinforce the OCD cycle.

The Rule-Making Mind

- I took seven minutes to call my doctor's office. I need to work an extra thirty minutes after clocking out to make up for it.

- A napkin flew off my plate during lunch, and I wasn't able to retrieve it. I need to clean litter off the road for an hour.

The urge to obey the dictates of the mind is overpowering when discomfort is present. **Public or private compulsions, such as those mentioned above, and self-deprecation may ensue.**

List some of the ways you have followed your mind's rules to find relief. How long did the resulting comfort last? Was it helpful in terms of what matters most in your life?

The Problem-Solving Machine

- It would've been better if I had kept my mouth shut!
- I'm a fraud because I can't get rid of these appalling thoughts.

Your mind is designed to be attentive to your circumstances and put in its two cents to help you avoid pain and suffering. It can find infinite reasons to lead you anywhere (e.g., ruminating about the past and future) but the present.

Below, list some of the solutions your mind suggests in relation to your scrupulosity OCD. When you act (i.e., compulsions) on them, are those solutions providing short-term or lasting results?

The Label-Making Mind

- I am unfaithful.
- I am a sinner.

When intrusive thoughts show up, the urge to harshly criticize and label yourself may seem helpful. After all, we human beings yearn for coherence (see pages 55 and 78)! But before long, those labels pop up all the time, and you start believing them. What are the labels that show up for you, and how productive and confident are you when you believe them? Write them down and how you feel after you begin to believe those labels.

The Fortune-Telling Machine

- What if I end up acting on my thoughts?
- What if I'm found out?

Your mind will provide every possible scenario in response to "what if" worry thoughts. It's easy to believe what your mind is predicting; after all, you have it right there, and, quite often, it does provide helpful advice. The problem is, can your mind really know the future? Sometimes you may say, "Well, based on experience, it may happen again." Sure it may, *but it may not*. You may feel hopeless and depressed when you believe your mind's predictions. Public and private compulsions may ensue.

What are the predictions your mind loves to make? Are you reacting as if they've already come to pass?

The Preachy Mind

- Did I really repent?
- How can I enjoy myself when there is so much suffering around me?

Do you feel like there is a strict preacher in your mind all day long? These types of thoughts may lead you to feel guilt and a constant urge to confess your "misdeeds" to your spiritual leader. You may not realize that confessing is actually a compulsion to comply with your preachy mind. There are those who decide to leave their faith, believing their faith has caused them to feel overwhelmed. They are not able to recognize it's the preachy mind at work.

Do you believe you have to follow the tenets of your religion and your values to perfection? What do you fear will happen if you don't obey the preachy mind?

Recognizing and acknowledging the mind for what it is
will enhance your mental flexibility and allow you to find peace.

5

Learning to Defuse from Internal Experiences

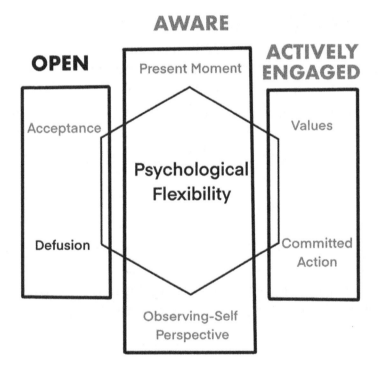

Fusion versus Defusion

Seth's Story

Whenever unwanted thoughts showed up for Seth, he would make a fist and hit himself. He would question his worth. "What do these thoughts say about me? Do I want them? Is that why they won't go away? If I don't fight against them, they may become reality. If I let them be in my head, it means I am as bad as if I were acting on them."

Seth's thoughts were the opposite of who he wanted to be. Because his thoughts were incongruent with his beliefs, he felt he should punish himself for having them. He did not recognize that the mere desire to punish himself was an indication that he, in fact, was not his thoughts.

One way he learned to develop psychological flexibility was through cognitive defusion skills. Before we dive into developing psychological flexibility through cognitive defusion skills, let's define *fusion* and *defusion*.

Fusion

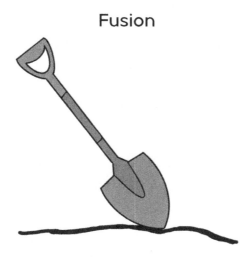

Often, various objects are fused to create tools. For example, a basic shovel is made up of at least three parts: the grip, the shaft, and the blade. For these parts to stay together, they are either welded or attached with screws. Though the shovel is presented as one object, it has parts that are combined, merged—or fused. Like the different parts of shovels are fused, we sometimes become fused with our thoughts, feelings, and other internal experiences.

Sometimes fusion can be helpful. When we become absorbed in reading a mystery novel or focus on certain tasks, like paying our taxes or taking a test, we are fused. These activities require our full attention, and that's a good thing!

But it is easy to become fused with painful thoughts. ("I'm bad because I cannot control those sexual images.") When we become fused with our thoughts and feelings, we may react as if they represent who we are.

We often forget that though our thoughts and other internal experiences are part of us, we are not those internal events.

The good news is that, unlike shovels, we can learn to defuse from our thoughts, feelings, and whatever else is occurring internally at any given moment!

Defusion

In order to create some distance between yourself and your unhelpful internal events, you can learn to **"defuse," or become unstuck, or unhooked**, from them. Once you defuse from difficult internal experiences, you can gently get back to the present moment and focus on what matters right then.

As you practice the exercises below, keep your top five values present. I share several exercises so you can try them all over time, and then choose the ones you find most useful when it comes to developing psychological flexibility.

Getting Unhooked

The scrupulous mind may, at times, feel like a monster who's fishing and "hooks" you as if you were a helpless fish trying to swim away only to get more entangled. When you get hooked, you may thrash around only to get caught in the scrupulosity trap. Hours may pass before you realize you've been hooked. Here is a practice that can help you respond differently.

Exercise 1. Acknowledge Getting Hooked[1]

After reading the instructions, set a timer for five minutes, then sit in a comfortable, quiet place and close your eyes. The purpose of this exercise is to help you notice when you get hooked (with thoughts, feelings, and other internal experiences) and then become unhooked (defused) accordingly.

- Focus on your breathing. Notice how the air enters your nostrils and expands your lungs as you breathe in. Focus on the warm air as it slowly exits your nostrils or mouth. As you pay attention to your breathing, say the word *breathing*.

- Soon enough, you will notice your attention drifting to something other than your breathing. When you become aware that you are no longer noticing your breathing, acknowledge it by saying, "Distracted," then gently refocus on your breathing.

- Be aware that your mind will distract you again. When you become aware that this has happened, say, "Distracted" and go back to breathing.

- At some point, you may notice a thought that leads you to start obsessing about a rule, judgment, memory, or future event and begin to feel distressed. That's the moment the scrupulosity monster has hooked you with a thought, feeling, or another internal event. You may forget you were in the middle of this practice. It happens. As soon as you realize it, acknowledge it by saying, "Hooked," then gently refocus on your breathing.

- Keep noticing until the timer goes off. You don't need to force yourself to think or feel. You just need to notice when you become distracted and hooked (by any experience such as a thought, memory, feeling, sensation, or urge). When you notice this has happened, acknowledge it as previously stated and gently bring your attention back to your breathing.

Every time you practice this exercise, write down what you've learned about you and your mind.

Exercise 2. Thoughts on Parade

Find a quiet place, read the instructions, and plan on doing this exercise for three to five minutes.

- Close your eyes when you are ready. Imagine you are standing on a sidewalk, watching a parade. The floats and people in the parade are carrying each thought that shows up in your mind.

- Watch the floats, and as you do, place each thought on a passing float. Try to envision people in costumes and marching bands with large banners carrying your thoughts, judgments, or memories. Perhaps there are large balloons. Feel free to place a thought on a balloon as well.

- It doesn't matter what or whom you choose to carry your thoughts. Just imagine your thoughts passing by with the parade.

- At one point during your five-minute practice, there may be a thought that hooks you, and you may forget you were doing this exercise. No worries. When you recognize this has happened, acknowledge it by saying, "Hooked," and gently go back to watching your thoughts on parade.

- What did you learn about your mind and yourself after practicing this exercise?

If watching your thoughts on a parade does not resonate with you, you can imagine watching your thoughts as if they were on clouds going by, sailboats, leaves on a stream, a conveyor belt at the airport, etc. You can decide what helps you notice your thoughts instead of being hooked by them.

Exercise 3. Sticky Notes for Sticky Thoughts

Those who do not have OCD have thoughts similar to those who struggle with OCD. These thoughts may be random, weird, disturbing, "immoral," unwanted, or distressing.[2] The difference is that for someone with OCD, those thoughts are stickier because the scrupulous mind tells them they shouldn't have them. And the more they try to get rid of them, the stickier they get. It is what they do with these thoughts that can create the challenge.

Read the instructions below and then practice this exercise. You'll need a few sticky notes. Think of at least four thoughts you struggle with the most and write one thought on each sticky note.

- Notice what internal experiences show up as you write down the thoughts you wish you didn't have. Place each sticky note on your forehead in a way that blocks your vision.

- If it were impossible to remove those sticky notes, they would be there all day long, obstructing your view and getting in the way of your daily tasks. Likewise, certain thoughts may be front and center in your mind and get in the way of you living life more meaningfully.

- Now, remove them and place them anywhere on your body—maybe on your arm, your shirt, or your lap. The sticky notes are still there, but they won't disrupt your daily tasks and what's most important to you. Even though they are still there, these thoughts and other internal experiences don't have to be the focus of every minute of your day.

- Are you willing to choose the sticky note containing the most disturbing thought and place it in your shirt or pants pocket, bag, backpack, or wallet and carry it around with you all day long?

- Notice what happens when you pull out the sticky note two or three times a day. Read it and acknowledge it with "There is that thought," then put it back.

- Then, when the thought pops up, acknowledge it by saying, "There it is. I'm not surprised" or "Thanks, Mind. I've got this," then pat your pocket or wallet, acknowledging its presence, and reconnect with what you were doing before the thought popped up.

This exercise will help you change your mental habits and recognize that you don't have to "control" the thought. It can be there, and you have more important things to do than obsess about it.

After doing this exercise several times, write about what you learned. How does acknowledging and defusing from your internal events help you live the values you listed in chapter 2?

Because ACT (acceptance and commitment therapy) is an exposure modality, these and subsequent exercises may feel difficult at first. Be patient and come back to the practices as you gain more understanding of the principles taught. These exercises will enable you to change your relationship with your internal experiences (e.g., thoughts, feelings, and sensations) so you can find peace, meaning, and joy.

> Though difficult thoughts and feelings may be present,
> they don't have to interrupt your daily life!

6

Being Open to Uncertainty

It is the mark of an educated mind to be able to entertain a thought without accepting it.

—Aristotle

Fear and Uncertainty in a River

Five minutes into the Naranjo River rapids in Costa Rica, the raft my son and his wife were in capsized, and I became fused with my thoughts and feelings: "Wow, glad they got back in and no one got stuck on a rock! I'm so scared. None of us should have come. What if my other sons or I get stuck in the rocks and are unable to get out and we drown?" The uncertainty and fear were excruciating.

Interestingly enough, I wasn't fused with my thoughts and feelings too long because the guide was continually yelling out instructions to help us maneuver our raft through the rapids. Since I didn't want to drown, I paid attention! My heart pounded, and my stomach hurt. I was afraid for my loved ones and myself. I wanted to run away from the situation, but I couldn't.

Whenever fear and uncertainty strike, your "helpful" mind will offer solutions to the problem, but, as we've discussed, these solutions are not effective in the long run. The uncertainty (e.g., whether God loves you, whether you are a good enough parent, whether you are perfectly honest) that prevails in the areas you care about most may lead you to feel hopeless.

How Can I Overcome Uncertainty?

Individuals struggling with scrupulosity OCD often ask how they can overcome uncertainty. But because uncertainty is part of the human experience, that question is unanswerable. I usually invite clients to ponder this question instead:

"How can I change my relationship with uncertainty?"

You may want to consider these follow-up questions:

- Is it possible my struggle is not with uncertainty itself but with the fact that I simply don't like it and cannot control the outcome and wish I could?

- What would life be like—not if uncertainty wasn't there but if I were willing to experience uncertainty even if I didn't like it?

Reassurance-Seeking: The Pervasive Compulsion

"What consumes your mind controls your life."

—*Anonymous*

Anthony's Story

Before treatment, Anthony believed he would eventually solve past experiences and be able to figure out whether, in fact, he had done something wrong. The uncertainty kept him awake at night. "Once I figure this out, I'll be able to move on!" The more he obsessed, the more his urge to look back seemed to intensify.

The following metaphor may give you a different perspective about the urge to look back in search of certainty.

The Magical Bank Metaphor[1]

Imagine you enter a competition and win a prize. Your bank account will receive daily deposits of $86,400, but there are a few stipulations:

1. You cannot transfer the money or give it away. Whatever you don't spend each day is taken away. However, every morning, your account receives another $86,400 for you to use.

2. The donor of the prize has the right to stop the deposits at any time, with very little notice. The transfers can be discontinued with you not being able to do anything about it. You might get a notification that simply says, "Sorry, your deposits have been suspended. You are done."

What would you do if you received such a prize, knowing the deposits could be interrupted at any time? What would you buy? What would you do? Would you purchase anything and everything you've always wanted? You would, wouldn't you? Not only would you spend it on yourself, you'd spend it on your loved ones and even strangers because, the reality is, you probably would not be able to spend it all on yourself, correct? You would want to spend every cent, wouldn't you?

Now, what if the prize you received was more precious than money?

Though we might not be able to see it clearly, we all have this magical bank. That magical bank is TIME! Every morning when we wake up, we are given 86,400 seconds as a gift, and when we go to sleep every night, we don't get credit for the time we didn't use.

When our day is over, we can't get it back. What time we didn't use is forever gone. We have our time account refilled every morning, but do we realize life is fragile and our account can be canceled anytime, without warning?

So, what will you do with your 86,400 seconds every day?

> Your time is precious, and you don't need to spend it on ineffective activities, such as obsessions and compulsions. Instead, you can acknowledge uncomfortable internal experiences and focus on the present moments of each and every day!

Consider your answers to these questions regularly:

- When I act on the urge to seek reassurance or give in to another compulsion, am I doing it for the sake of my values or the scrupulous mind?
- Are my compulsions strengthening my relationship with my loved ones and God?
- Am I able to regularly notice how uncertainty is propelling my urge to behave compulsively?
- How have my religious activities become a checklist?
- Are my behaviors a source of spiritual and emotional strength or the means to relieve uncertainty, anxiety, and guilt?
- Are my religious practices done in moderation or with rigidity?

Private and Public Reassurance-Seeking Compulsions

Kristina's Story

Kristina struggled with religious and moral anxiety, but she never could be certain whether she was actually struggling with it or using it as an excuse. She'd often ask her therapist whether she really had scrupulosity OCD. "Are you sure I have scrupulosity OCD? What if it is something else? What if I'm using it as an excuse? What if I actually end up acting on my thoughts? Are you sure these thoughts are normal?"

These are common questions among OCD sufferers. The need for certainty seems to be the focus for those who struggle with scrupulosity as well as other subsets of OCD.

Your fears may compel you to constantly look for reassurance. Your yearning for coherence with your thoughts can lead you to cease doing those activities that bring you joy. ("I wish I could be with my friends, but my lustful thoughts may show up, so I'd better stay home.") Uncertainty is unpleasant and naturally creates other uncomfortable internal experiences. Reassurance-seeking is the easiest path. Even though you may not realize it, private compulsions may be your current go-to rituals to find relief.

Below are examples of private and public reassurance-seeking compulsions.

Private Reassurance-Seeking Compulsions

- You try to rationalize or dissect your thoughts, feelings, and behaviors.
- You constantly question your character and beliefs because your thoughts do not align with the type of person you're striving to become.
- You try to figure out what else you need to do even after you've repented and made restitution because you continue to feel anxious and uncertain no matter what you do.
- You try to figure out what led you to feel guilty.

Public Reassurance-Seeking Compulsions

- Combing the internet and reading books and other material to verify you are not what your thoughts say you may be.
- Texting, emailing, or calling someone to feel reassured. ("Jess, do you think I'm a bad person?")
- Constantly asking family, friends, and faith leaders to help you find relief from guilt, anxiety, shame, uncertainty, and other emotions. This can be in the form of "confessing" your thoughts or asking questions to find relief.
- Giving in to other unhelpful behaviors that aren't strengthening your faith and/or values and doing them mainly to find relief.

The Doors of Uncertainty

Looking for certainty can feel like facing a bunch of closed doors with signs that invite you to open them so you can find certainty once and for all.

The scrupulous mind seems to say, "If you confess your sin one more time (open that next door), you'll know for sure that you are forgiven." You know the feeling.

What happens once you open that door? There will be another question, and another, and another. Although the uncertainty never goes away, you can start learning to embrace uncertainty by acknowledging the doubt.

Exercise 1. Acknowledge Uncertainty

Find a quiet place to sit and practice this exercise. Imagine you are walking along a hallway lined with closed doors on your right and left, then think of a situation that consistently brings you uncertainty.

Imagine placing the doubt on each door. Acknowledge what's happening: "I'm having the thought _____." Then acknowledge that you are noticing you are having that thought," as shown below.

- I may cause my kids' death.
- **I'm having the thought,** "I may cause my kids' death."
- **I'm noticing I'm having the thought,** "I may cause my kids' death."

- I am so anxious!
- **I'm having** the feeling of anxiety.
- **I'm noticing I'm having** the feeling of anxiety.

- I feel like I'm drowning on dry land.
- **I'm having** the bodily sensation of drowning on dry land.
- **I'm noticing I'm having** the bodily sensation of drowning on dry land.

- I want to triple-check the brakes on my car.
- **I'm having** the urge to triple-check the brakes on my car.
- **I'm noticing I'm having** the urge to triple-check the brakes on my car.

Do you see the difference? You can become an observer by looking *at* the thoughts and other internal events instead of looking *from* them.

Write down the doubts you experience every day, then add the phrase, "I'm having _____," then "I'm noticing I'm having _____." You can acknowledge the mind this way throughout the day.

> Whenever uncertainty is present,
> acknowledge it instead of getting hooked by it!

Recommendations to Decrease Reassurance-Seeking

1. Keep a reassurance-seeking log. Tally the times you look for reassurance for a day or two to get a baseline for this compulsion, then decide to decrease the urge to find certainty. For example, if your baseline shows you seek reassurance twenty times a day, try to decrease it to fifteen or less.

2. List your reassurance-seeking questions. Write down the most common questions you want reassurance for. As new questions arise, add them to the list. Then, as the urge to seek reassurance arises, check-mark it to acknowledge it. When a new question arises, write it down and check-mark it when it shows up again. Do so throughout the day and week. By writing and check-marking it, you are acknowledging it. As you do this, you can also silently say, "There it is again. Thanks, Mind. You may be right. I don't know." Then gently reconnect with what you were doing.

3. Delay, limit, change, or replace reassurance-seeking behaviors (private or public compulsions) by using the defusion skills you've learned so far. As you learn more skills, implement them instead of giving in to the scrupulous mind.

4. Be creative as you modify this unhelpful behavior. For example, if you usually call or text a close relative or friend, seeking reassurance ("Was I rude to you yesterday?" "Do you think God is really forgiving?"), practice cognitive defusion skills ("I'm noticing I'm having the feeling of uncertainty." "I'm noticing I'm having the urge to seek reassurance.") to help you delay the compulsions.

5. Instead of giving in to reassurance-seeking compulsions, write down your questions as if you were going to mail (snail mail) them to someone. Mail them if you really need to. The goal is for you to teach your mind that you won't abide by its rules or follow its impractical, overprotective advice.

You have a choice when it comes to what you do despite the scrupulous mind's insistence on *unnecessarily* keeping you safe because there is no fire or tiger threatening you at the moment.

Support from Loved Ones

Because clinical scrupulosity involves obsessions and compulsions surrounding faith and morality, it can be missed and misunderstood. Family members, friends, and faith leaders may interpret your scrupulosity as devotion and inadvertently reinforce your obsessions and compulsions by giving you reassurance every time you ask for it.

Even so, they are interested in your well-being and *can* be there for you as you journey through the turbulent waters of OCD. You don't have to do this alone! Share what you are learning and doing to live more meaningfully. The information below will help you and those interested in your welfare to distinguish between the compulsions and the legitimate need for information.

Distinguishing Information-Seeking and Reassurance Seeking[2]

An Information-Seeker:	A Reassurance-Seeker:
Asks a question once	Repeatedly asks the same question
Asks questions to be informed	Asks questions to feel less anxious
Accepts the answer provided	Responds to an answer by challenging the answerer, arguing, or insisting the answer be repeated or rephrased
Asks people who are qualified to answer the question	Often asks the question of those unqualified to answer it
Asks answerable questions	Often asks unanswerable questions
Seeks the truth	Seeks a desired answer
Accepts relative, qualified, or uncertain answers when appropriate	Insists on absolute, definitive answers, whether appropriate or not
Pursues only the information necessary to form a conclusion or make a decision	Indefinitely pursues information without ever forming a conclusion or making a decision

Permission to print granted by Alec Pollard.

You and your loved ones need to know the difference between a compulsion and truly asking for information. Your loved ones can help you decrease this pervasive, unhelpful behavior. You need emotional support, and the best way for them to give you that support is to listen to you and acknowledge your feelings instead of giving you reassurance. They can also show patience, empathy, and compassion.

Don't feel like you cannot talk to them at all. It's okay to seek support. When it comes to OCD, you can say something like, "My scrupulosity is getting to me today." They can then acknowledge that you are struggling and help you through it without giving you reassurance. They can ask you to share what skills would be helpful for you right now. Teaching them the skills lets you review, practice, and reinforce what you've learned.

Since you are aiming for flexibility, your loved ones can focus on that as well. When you absolutely need reassurance because the only other option is to end up in the hospital with a panic attack, by all means, let them give you the reassurance you need.

When they give you reassurance under those circumstances, they can still remind you that this will strengthen the OCD. They can then provide limited reassurance. As you become more flexible, you will no longer need to find reassurance from anyone, including yourself.

Choose one of the five recommendations discussed in this section to decrease reassurance-seeking behaviors and practice it for the next few days. Write it down, and after a few days, write about what you've learned.

> Someday, we may find certainty and
> the elusive pot of gold at the end of the rainbow.
> For now, let's focus on what we can control–
> choosing how to respond to difficult internal events.

Responding to the Overprotective Mind

Uncertainty is part of life. No one is spared from it, but if you struggle with scrupulosity OCD, having doubts about what matters most to you (i.e., your values) can be tormenting. You may feel stuck and like others don't understand the pain you're experiencing.

The good news is that as you become aware of the scrupulous mind's default function (to protect you), you can respond differently than you have in the past.

The Mind Is Like an Overprotective, Well-Meaning Grandma

When I think of the human mind, I think of my four-foot, ten-inch tall maternal grandmother. The difficulties and joys she experienced taught her much about life. She was raised by a rigid, overprotective maternal aunt and likewise wished to protect her loved ones from danger and mistreatment. Her constant reminders to ensure everyone was safe could be tiring. "Take your sweater or you'll catch a cold." "Get home before dark. Nothing good happens after dark!"

She was awesome, but she was a worrier. Her advice was well intended, but she didn't have all the information about the world in which her grand- and great-grandchildren were being raised. Her life experience growing up in Guatemala was different.

We all learned that arguing with her was useless. When she would give us her well-meaning advice, instead of rationalizing or arguing with her, we'd play along. "Thanks, Grandma. I'm listening." My dear grandma had a one-track mind. She only wanted to protect us from future pain—just like the mind does!

Instead of arguing with your mind, play along by thanking and acknowledging it. Otherwise, you can get stuck in an argument that won't take you anywhere.

This practice will help you get unhooked from the content of your thoughts and become more open to uncertainty.

Exercise 2. Cognitive Defusion Phrases with Uncertainty

Familiarize yourself with the following examples of how you can thank and acknowledge your mind, then list the thoughts the scrupulous mind produces. Invite a loved one to help you practice responding to your mind. Your loved one can play the role of your mind producing the thought, and you can answer with a cognitive defusion statement that contains a flavor of uncertainty as shown in the examples below. Give your loved one a list of your most common worries so they can effectively role-play your mind.

a. Acknowledge your mind by genuinely thanking it when it produces overprotective, unhelpful thoughts. Then add uncertainty.

Unhelpful Thought	Genuinely Thank Your Mind, then Add Uncertainty
"You may harm someone today!"	"Thanks, Mind! You are worrying about me as usual. We'll just have to see."
"Others can probably tell you're a hypocrite."	"I hear you, Mind. Thanks!"

Examples of Uncertainty Phrases
Perhaps.
We'll have to see.
I don't know.
You may be right.
That's possible.
I may never know for sure.

List the thoughts your mind constantly produces. Write down how you plan to genuinely acknowledge and thank your mind as you go about your day. Remember that your mind means well, but its advice may not be useful.

Unhelpful Thought	Genuinely Thank Your Mind, then Add Uncertainty

b. Acknowledge your mind by playing along with it and adding phrases of uncertainty.

Unhelpful Thought	Play Along with Your Mind, then Add Uncertainty
"You're not worthy of God's blessings."	"You may be right. We'll see!"
"You don't deserve your family's love."	"You have a point, Mind. I might never know."

List the thoughts your mind constantly produces. Write down how you plan to acknowledge your mind by playing along with it.

Unhelpful Thought	Play Along with Your Mind, then Add Uncertainty

After acknowledging the mind with a phrase of uncertainty, you can gently shift your attention back to the present—to whatever you were doing before the thought showed up. The more you practice, the more creative you'll be when responding to your mind.

Do not argue with or try to justify to your mind what you are doing or plan on doing. It's best to just play along as I did with my grandma.

As you continue to practice defusion skills and acknowledging your mind, you'll start viewing thoughts and feelings of uncertainty with a different mindset. Your scrupulous mind may insist you need to live your faith and other values perfectly. You have a choice (see graphic) on how to respond to your internal experiences in each moment.

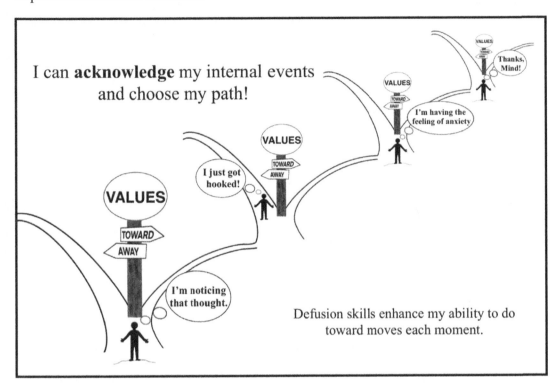

> Change does not happen overnight.
> It's up to us to take the time to develop new neural pathways.
> If we don't, everything will stay the same.

7

Taking What's Being Offered Now

If you aren't willing to have it, you will.

—*Steven C. Hayes*

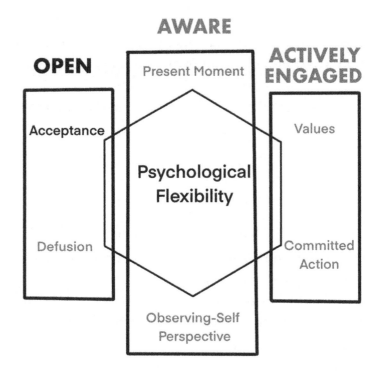

Lisa's Story

At the beginning of the COVID pandemic, Lisa's scrupulous mind led her to obsess about whether she would be responsible for someone's death. She was overwhelmed with thoughts such as "What if I have COVID and contaminated my kids' teacher yesterday? She'll contaminate everyone else at school. Hundreds of people could be sick or die because of me!" Her inflated sense of responsibility was off the charts. Her obsessions and compulsions began to get in the way of her relationships with family and friends. It seemed she was experiencing scrupulosity storms all day long.

What Is Your Default Reaction during Scrupulosity Storms?

Notice if you are engaging in any of the following instinctual behaviors to keep your unpleasant thoughts and feelings at bay.

Escaping

Are you engaging in ineffective behaviors like DOTS (see page 44)? "If you distract yourself and avoid life, the emotional pain will disappear," the mind may whisper.

What do you notice about your body and yourself when you are trying to escape?

Fighting

You may say, "I'll fight this darn illness! I won't let OCD get in my way!" Naturally, you want to live with joy and resilience and not let OCD get in the way. However, "fighting," as in resisting the obsessions and compulsions, is not helpful. Whether the compulsions are public or private, the more you resist (by arguing with your mind or any other way) or fight them (hence, concentrate on them), the more you'll have them.

When I use the word *fight* in this workbook, I am referring to the human instinct to resist distressing internal experiences (i.e., thoughts, memories, judgments, feelings, sensations, and urges). When you resist or fight these internal events, what do you notice happening in your body and yourself?

Surrendering

You may want to submit to the scrupulous mind. It is the easiest path. The painful feelings and sensations may subside momentarily. You may hope the respite lasts longer the next time. You may be ready to give up, resigned to feeling miserable the rest of your life.

When you experience this mindset, notice what happens in your body and yourself.

Rigidly Enduring

Sometimes you may decide you're going to face your fears once and for all. Trying to endure is a good start. The problem is that you don't know exactly how to be open to the discomfort. Though you are trying, you may still be missing out on living with joy and purpose because white-knuckling internal events can leave you feeling exhausted.

What is it like when you spend your day white-knuckling your feelings and other internal experiences?

No worries! There is a better way to respond to your emotions. It is called **willingness.**

The willingness exercises in this chapter will allow you navigate the unpleasant internal experiences, let go of fear, and start doing what matters most in your life. Please don't be in a hurry. You may want to choose one exercise per week or month. Learning to be open to unpleasant internal experiences (e.g., thoughts and feelings) is a process.

Taking What's Being Offered Now

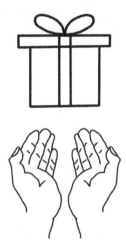

If you received a gift from your best friend, you would probably accept it even if it were something you already had or didn't like, right? You would say thank you and get back to visiting and doing what mattered in that moment.

The word *acceptance* is often misunderstood. Sometimes people believe that acceptance means *forever* becoming the victim of your circumstances.

Acceptance, or willingness, means having an open mind and yielding to what is presented (e.g., the internal experiences—thoughts, emotions, memories, sensations, and urges) **to you in that moment so you can keep moving toward what really matters in your life**. You cannot fight a natural event, like rain, nor can you fight natural events like feelings, sensations, and urges.

To Hide or Open Up—That's the Question

When we feel threatened, our natural inclination is to hide from the danger we perceive. During my white-water rafting adventure, I often cowered in the raft, white-knuckling the situation and hoping it would be over! When you feel anxiety and uncertainty, you can tell your mind, "Buddy, there is no lion, fire, or white water swirling around me, even though it feels like it. Thanks for your concern."

When you get triggered and worry thoughts (obsessions) and unpleasant feelings arise, you have a choice. Let's explore some options:

Exercise 1. Being on the Defense

- Take a minute to physically place your body in a defensive posture, as if a gigantic, disgusting, intimidating creature were crawling toward you. What would your attitude and demeanor be? If you were trying to shield yourself from harm, would you hide under your bed, desk, or chair, hoping the monster couldn't see you? Go ahead and take a moment to adopt that defensive stance.

    How do you feel when you assume a defensive posture?

- Next, set your alarm for two minutes. Take in your surroundings, then notice an object in the room, and as you notice it, say **no**[1] to it, meaning, "It has to change. It's unacceptable. I want it gone right now!" Keep noticing one object at a time and saying **no** in a rigid and defensive posture until the alarm goes off.

    Write about how you felt and what you learned. Did you feel tense?

- Lastly, set your alarm for another two minutes. Use your smartphone to find words, images, sounds, or anything that may trigger the scrupulous mind to come to the rescue and advise you to say **no** with a defensive and fearful posture. Say **no** (in a fearful and defensive way) to any thought, memory, judgment, feeling, sensation, and urge that shows up in the next two minutes.

    Write about what this was like for you. Did you feel stressed at some point? Your mind may say, "That's exactly my advice: say no and you'll be okay!" The question is, will you choose to listen to the scrupulous mind and become rigid? When you do, does that response work for you?

Exercise 2. Adopting a "Bring It On!" Stance

- Now, think about the way you would act if a monster were coming toward you, and though you were scared, the monster was blind and could only smell your fear. Think about what your posture would look like if you were to say, "Bring it on!" Go ahead. Get into a confident pose. Write about your experience.

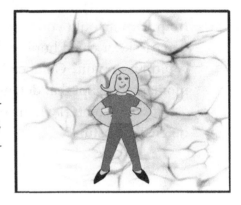

- Next, set your alarm for two minutes, then look around the room, find an object, and say yes to it. Notice how it feels to say yes in a confident and flexible manner. Meaning, "Yes, that's okay. I don't have to change it. I can accept it for what it is. I can allow it as it is. Keep noticing one object at a time and saying yes[2] until the alarm goes off. Write about your insights.

- Last, set your alarm for three to five minutes and write down a thought you wish you didn't have. The scrupulous mind may advise you to say, "No! If you do, it may come true!" or "You are a bad person for purposely thinking about it and writing it down!" Can you be willing to face (i.e., exposure) the unpleasant internal events that accompany the thought for a few moments?

  Instead of trying to push the thought away, acknowledge the mind and say yes (meaning, "I hear you, Mind"). Let your mind talk, and respond with a confident "Yes!" (you are acknowledging the mind with confidence). Notice any uncomfortable thoughts or other internal experiences that show up (e.g., memories, judgments, feelings, sensations, urges) and continue to respond with a yes until the alarm goes off. Write about what it felt like doing this exercise with a yes, or confident mindset.

Though your mind may advise you to fight, escape, or surrender, you know this well-meaning advice is coming from an overprotective mind. The advice is short-lived! When you adopt an open and curious stance, you are dropping the fight with the scrupulous mind and moving toward living with flexibility and joy.

Invitation

See if you can practice a confident stance every day, as often as possible. When you notice you are reacting defensively, instead, say yes to the thought and other internal events that show up. "In this moment, I choose to say yes!"

You may be surprised at how, over time, this exercise can help you build confidence even in the face of difficult internal experiences.

Feeling Fearful and Accepting What Is

Accept—then act. Whatever the present moment contains, accept it as if you had chosen it. Always work with it, not against it. . . . This will miraculously transform your whole life.

—Eckhart Tolle[3]

One summer, while snorkeling in the ocean, I learned a valuable lesson regarding willingness to **take what is offered in the moment**. My snorkeling story illustrates **how easily we forget to let go of the fight we cannot win.**

While swimming toward the area of a lagoon that had a reef near the open ocean, I became enthralled with my surroundings and let the ocean current take me wherever it went. After a few minutes of enjoying the fish, I lifted my head above the water to discover the current had taken me out of the lagoon and into the open ocean, fortunately not too far from the lagoon—yet.

The Alarm

The second I realized I was not in the lagoon, my vigilant mind quickly alerted me: "Oh no! This is dangerous. I've got to get back in." I proceeded to swim back toward the lagoon. After what seemed like a long time, though it was probably just a minute, I realized I was not making headway and was caught in a current. It may also have been because I'm not the best swimmer!

I thought, "I cannot get tired," so I floated and rested. When I began to swim back, I spotted my sister about thirty feet away and yelled, "I can't get back in!" She responded, "You can do it." I yelled back, "I'm trying to, but the current is too strong!" I tried to do the backstroke but went the wrong way. She swam a little closer and reminded me to stay calm and slow down. Frustrated, I answered, "I know! I'm trying!"

Fusion

I had become totally fused with my thoughts and was trying to swim as fast as I could to get out of the current taking me away from the lagoon. The problem-solving machine inside my head was telling me to do so to keep me safe. **I got entangled in the content of my thoughts:** "I am out of the lagoon. I am past the safety ropes. I'm in danger. There is no lifeguard. No one noticed me drifting away. What would've happened if my sister had not seen me? The fish were nice but not worth drowning for. This is too hard!" My protector was at work. There was no storm. The current was strong but not powerful enough to make it impossible to get back in if I was willing to accept where I was in that moment. But I felt icky. My body was in a fight-or-flight response.

Willingness

The moment I got caught up in the meaning of my thoughts was the moment I began to fight. I was not willing to be outside the lagoon, though it was no deeper than the farthest areas of the lagoon. Thankfully, I recognized the unhelpful thoughts and was able to connect and embrace the actuality of being outside of the lagoon.

No matter what I did in frantic mode, my reality was not going to change. When I embraced my situation and allowed my emotions and sensations to be there, I was able to think more clearly instead of panicking.

When I was desperately trying to remove myself from the situation, I didn't get anywhere. Once I let go of the fight with my internal experiences, I was able to let them take their natural course.

Instead of reacting frantically and fixating on just the end goal—getting back inside the lagoon to feel safe—my focus became one slow breaststroke (my version of a breaststroke) at a time. I realized that the current wasn't that strong, and I was able to get back to shore.

Invitation

When uncertainty and other unpleasant external or internal events show up, you can learn to be **willing to take what is offered in that instant and let your emotions and physical sensations take their course.** The effort and time you spend fighting them can be channeled toward cultivating and acting on living a richer, more meaningful life.

> You can be open to what is in the moment, even when the *flesh is weak*. Be patient, though—it requires time and practice.

Exercise 3. Accepting Your Emotions and Bodily Sensations[4]

The following exercises will help you learn how to embrace difficult emotions and bodily sensations one step at a time.

Read the instructions first or record the instructions on your smartphone. I recommend you practice them as often as you can, so that when furious or mild scrupulosity storms arise, you can respond accordingly.

Taking a Curious Stance

Think of a situation related to your scrupulosity that brings up intense feelings (e.g., uncertainty, anxiety, guilt, etc.) and the sensations (e.g., tightness in your abdomen, pit in your stomach, etc.) being manifested in your body.

- When you are ready, close your eyes and acknowledge how you are feeling in general. ("I'm feeling awful.")

- Slowly scan your body from head to toe, locating the bodily sensation related to the emotion.

- Imagine yourself as a curious scientist examining this bodily sensation and noticing where it is located. If this sensation were a tangible object, what would it look like? What color and shape would it have? Give it a shape and imagine the color of this sensation in this moment. If you could touch it, what would be its texture and temperature? If it made sounds, what sounds would it make? If it had vibrations, where would they begin and end within your body?

- Continue observing the bodily sensation (rapid heart rate, sweating, nausea, etc.) that has been brought on by the feeling (e.g., uncertainty, anxiety, guilt, etc.) as if you were a curious scientist looking inside your body. Imagine noticing the feeling manifested in your body a few more moments, and when you're ready, open your eyes.

- Take a moment to draw this particular feeling manifested in your body. It shows up regularly in your life, so find out what it's like to objectify it. Then write your insights after drawing it. Next time it shows up, see if you can *observe* the bodily sensation as a thing instead of *trying to get rid* of it.

Next, you'll practice how to acknowledge and allow the bodily sensation with the ABCDE steps.

Acknowledge the Mind

- After observing the uncomfortable bodily sensation as if you were a curious scientist, acknowledge (defuse or unhook from) the internal experiences that come to your awareness; e.g., "I'm noticing the feeling of

_____ (anxiety, anger, sadness, etc.)." "I'm noticing the bodily sensation of _____ (rapid heart rate, sweating, nausea, etc.)."

- Your mind won't stay quiet during your practices or daily life. Continue to acknowledge this during this practice. ("There goes my mind again. Thanks, Mind.")

Breathe

- Notice your breathing. Slowly breathe in and out. As you exhale, picture the air flowing into the area of your body where you have located the unpleasant sensation related to the emotion that is present in the moment.

- Continue to breathe in slowly, and as you exhale, imagine the air flowing around the bodily sensation. Do not misunderstand this step. You are **not** trying to breathe the sensation away. Just notice your breathing and imagine the air flowing around the area where you are noticing the sensation in your body.

- Do this whenever you feel the unpleasant sensation. As you continue to breathe around it, remember to have a curious-scientist stance.

Create Space for the Sensation

- As you continue breathing, imagine creating space for the sensation in your body as you breathe out. Life has offered you this sensation related to a feeling in this moment. Allow it by expanding that area with your breath.

- The sensation may grow bigger and stronger or smaller and weaker. Just notice what it does and keep breathing around the sensation to make room for it.

Decide to Allow the Sensation

- You are the only one who can decide to allow the bodily sensation to carry out its function in this moment. You can choose to either allow it or fight it, and you know what happens when you fight it. Trying to resist something built into your system only leads to frustration and further entanglement.

- Observe it and let it take its natural course without pushing it away.

- Sometimes you'll notice a new feeling or sensation surfacing. Repeat the steps above as needed.

Engage in What Matters Most

- When you feel compelled to resist your thoughts and feelings, does that help you become the person you want to be? Why not spend your precious time and energy on what matters instead of battling your internal experiences?

- When the urge is irresistible and you do something to find relief, does that take you closer to who and what matters most in your life? Your values, not the scrupulous mind, can be your guide.

Learning to embrace your emotions and accompanying bodily sensations can be difficult at first, but don't give up.

As you continue to practice these steps, you will feel empowered and gain more confidence in your relationship with the unpleasant emotions and bodily sensations that naturally come and go in your life.

Let's review the process. First, take a curious-scientist approach as you locate and objectify the bodily sensation. Next, follow the ABCDE steps:

- **A**cknowledge your thoughts and other internal events.
- **B**reathe around the area where the uncomfortable sensation is located.
- **C**reate space for the sensation.
- **D**ecide to allow the sensation to carry on with its function.
- **E**ngage in what matters.

Repeat the steps as often as you'd like.

If you'd like to listen to a similar narration on YouTube, you can find it here: https://www.youtube.com/watch?v=JBZyROaDtZw.

Julia's Story

When Julia learned her boss had COVID, the fleeting thought, *If my boss dies, I could move up to his position*, showed up. She felt horrible for having that thought and spent hours obsessing to find certainty that she absolutely didn't wish her boss any harm. Sadly, she eventually left a good-paying job to reassure herself she didn't want her boss's position or death.

Whenever you feel overwhelmed and discouraged because you simply cannot embrace the uncertainty your worries bring up, try this practice.

Exercise 4. Embracing Uncertainty as You Would a Child[5]

Take a few slow, deep breaths for a few moments. Then imagine holding uncertainty as you would a newborn child who is crying (or any defenseless creature who is hurt). Imagine looking at uncertainty with compassion and patience. Allow the feeling to be right there. Embrace the doubt gently. If you are willing, place your hands on the area of your body where you feel it. Imagine gently holding uncertainty for just a few more moments.

Uncertainty storms can leave you feeling exhausted. Despite your efforts, you may be disappointed in yourself because you gave in to a compulsion. You may be caught up in unhelpful internal events. Do not give up. Remember your reason to keep going (i.e., values) and how you'll keep doing what matters most to you!

Exercise 5. Embrace Uncertainty in the Areas of Life (Life Domains) You May Have Neglected

Are there areas of your life you have forgotten to cultivate because you've been too busy trying to find certainty?

Below is a list of the most relevant life domains. Rank them from one to five with five being the least important for you at this time.

Life Domains	Rank
Relationships	
Education/Work	
Personal Growth/Health	
Spirituality	
Recreation/Leisure	

In the chart below, write down two areas you'd like to participate in even when painful internal experiences are present. Then choose the value you want to live in those areas as well as the behaviors you wish to act upon despite the uncertainty.

For example, you may choose work (see chart below). You might value leadership. However, you might avoid speaking up during staff meetings because your mind says you're an impostor and don't deserve your position.

At your next staff meeting, you may choose to embrace uncertainty and speak up. As shown, you can implement defusion and willingness skills ("I am noticing the thought I am an impostor. Thanks, Mind. I can create space for this discomfort right now.") and then gently shift your attention back to the meeting.

You can also write down what you've learned from this activity, which is what we call an "exposure." **Exposures will help you practice willingness and other flexibility skills so you can live a values-focused life instead of being stuck in the scrupulosity trap.** For example, you can acknowledge, "I'm learning to be comfortable with the discomfort because I want to connect with God."

Choose the domain you'd like to work on, the value you want to live in that domain, the activity where you will embrace uncertainty (exposure), the skills you'll apply, and what you learned by living your values even when discomfort was present.

Life Domain	Value	Activity to Embrace Despite Uncertainty	Skills Used	What I Learned
Work	Leadership	Speaking up at staff meetings	Noticing and acceptance skills	I can live my values despite discomfort.

Life Domain	Value	Activity to Embrace Despite Uncertainty	Skills Used	What I Learned

What am I learning as I actively engage in what matters most?

Ponder these questions:

- What things that I value have I neglected?

- What have I missed because I often get caught in the scrupulosity trap?

- Have there been any losses in my relationships, education/work, personal growth/health, spirituality, and recreation/leisure because I've been pointlessly trying to satisfy the scrupulous mind and my uncertainty?

- What activities am I currently avoiding that I used to enjoy?

- Which domain will I work on next, and why does that domain matter to me?

Points to Remember

- Everyone experiences unhelpful thoughts, feelings, and sensations and gets fused with them at one time or another. But when you have OCD, all internal events are magnified and you become stuck with them longer.
- Beware of using any of the skills taught in this workbook as compulsions. The goal for practicing these skills is **NOT** to avoid, resist, fight, or get rid of the thoughts, memories, judgments, feelings, sensations, and urges.
- The goal is for you to create space between you and the internal experiences that get you stuck in the scrupulosity trap. When you are able to defuse and create space for those painful internal events, you are taking steps toward developing psychological flexibility and finding joy.

Note

The next chapter addresses faith challenges you might have with religious scrupulosity.

8
Addressing Dilemmas of Faith

Dan's Story

Whenever Dan prayed, his attention drifted within seconds, and he felt guilty for not staying focused. And when he didn't follow his scrupulous mind's rules ("Your prayer has to be perfect!"), his anxiety and guilt went through the roof. He believed his guilt meant a Higher Power was trying to tell him he "should" pray again until it was perfect. He often felt frustrated, saying, "I feel like God is displeased with me? I should pray again."

Prayers of Gratitude

> *He is a wise man who does not grieve for the things which he has not, but rejoices for those which he has.*
>
> —Epictetus[1]

It may be difficult to feel grateful when you're struggling, but it has been shown that individuals who wish to boost their level of happiness can do so by altering the way they relate to their lives. It is not what happens in life but how we respond to life that matters![2]

Gratitude is an attitude that can be learned and alter our physical and emotional well-being. Individuals who practice gratitude "tend to feel more happy, hopeful, vital, and satisfied with their lives, while being less materialistic, and envious of others' success."[3]

If you feel guilty because you haven't been grateful, acknowledge and allow that feeling in this moment. Consider changing prayers dictated by the preachy mind to meaningful prayers.

Will you consider making your daily prayers about gratitude and compassion instead of confessions or petitions? Is Divinity aware of your actions and most importantly your suffering? Ponder your answer.

Prayers of Uncertainty

Allowing for uncertainty in life is like stepping into turbulent white-water rapids. When it comes to uncertainty, you can hold on to your faith and spiritual beliefs to help you get back on course. Your faith is an essential part of your life; don't let the scrupulous mind get in the way.

- Notice if you are praying to satisfy the scrupulous mind or to communicate and feel God's love.

- When your mind tells you to confess, instead of listing all your mistakes and possible sins as you pray, acknowledge the mind by using cognitive defusion phrases with uncertainty. ("I hear you, Mind. Yes. I may be unworthy. Thanks.")

- Whether you've sinned or not, do you need to continually ask for forgiveness? Notice if your confessing and repenting behaviors are in the service of connecting and strengthening your relationship with the Almighty or if you're doing these things to appease the scrupulous mind.

    You may want to instead say, "God, you know my thoughts and behaviors." Then acknowledge your blessings and finish your prayer without confessing every detail or repeating anything. Most likely, your level of anxiety or guilt will rise because you didn't listen to the preachy mind. Acknowledge whatever emotion you feel, and create space for your internal experiences.

- Pray on your terms, not the scrupulous mind's terms. The goal is to refrain from giving in to any compulsions. Set a time limit on your prayers. Use the skills you've learned so far.

Instead of obsessively and compulsively praying to confess your sins to God, remember your beliefs. Does God love you unconditionally despite your struggles with scrupulosity OCD?

When you pray, consider these points:

- Does God need to hear every single fact about my sins or perceived wrongful doings every time I pray? What am I hoping to accomplish?

- Do I hope the Creator will see me differently? Why?

- Is it possible that my prayers are related to my being hooked with difficult internal experiences? Am I praying to find relief?

- Are my religious habits strengthening my relationship with the Creator?

Exercise 1. "Hello, Old Friend!"

Uncertainty is like an annoying old friend. It visits too frequently, and you don't like it. And while it's present, why not acknowledge it? Whenever it shows up, begin to notice your breathing. Purposely take slow, deep breaths. As you take a deep breath, say, "Hello." As you exhale say, "Old friend." Continue to do so and allow uncertainty to be in this moment.

> Breathe in—"Hello." Breathe out—"Old friend."

Take a few moments to make room for this old friend. By breathing uncertainty in (or other feelings) and allowing it to stay, you're reminding yourself that this is a better option than trying to push it away and getting stuck in the scrupulosity trap. The feeling is going to be present anyway—might as well open up to it and enhance your psychological flexibility.

Although you may find the above exercise calming as you allow your "old friend" to be there, this could lead you to start using it as a way to find relief. Remember, beware of using this and other skills as compulsions.

Is the Holy Spirit Absent?

Jim's Story

Jim reported he had been a faithful believer but began questioning his faith. He felt discouraged and hopeless and attributed his emotions to what he perceived as unworthiness. No matter how faithfully he tried to live, he couldn't feel the Holy Spirit's presence in his life.

There are many, like Jim, who report feeling this painful void. You are not alone. Every devoted human being will at times question their faith. However, if you struggle with OCD, the doubts are magnified, and you can become stuck in the scrupulosity trap when you want them gone.

If you didn't have doubts what would you be doing with respect to your faith and daily life? Would you instead be willing to do those things that you value even in the presence of uncertainty? Are you willing to be curious and find out what may happen as you do it with a flexible mindset?

The Hands Metaphor

After reading this sentence, cover your eyes, walk around the room without peeking, and come back to your reading.

If you had to live life with your hands stuck to your eyes, it would be difficult to go about your daily tasks, wouldn't it? Now, stretch your arms and hands as far from your face as you can. Do it as if you were trying to remove them. Well, you cannot. If you went about trying to remove your arms and hands, this behavior would distract you from doing the things that mattered, wouldn't it?

Like your arms and hands, your internal events are part of you. When you go about life trying to remove them, you're letting that get in the way of what's important to you (e.g., connecting with God).

No worries. You are learning psychological flexibility to help you find peace and hope in your journey!

Decisions, Faith, and Uncertainty

Brennan's Story

Brennan strove his best to live his religious beliefs. He didn't want to make a bad decision and risk hurting someone or offending God. When dating, he wanted to be sure he dated the "right" person and that God approved. There were times he feared losing his faith. "If I abandon my faith, will that be the right decision?" When feeling anxious and uncertain, he'd think, "This must be a sign I am making a bad decision." The more he worried about making the right choice, the more doubtful he became.

Consider these questions:

- How often do I compulsively check for the "right feeling" so I can make a decision?
- Am I willing to make a decision and trust that with God's help, I will be able to adjust, even when the outcome is not what I expected?
- Am I able to remember that feelings and thoughts are not facts and that the scrupulous mind is pulling me into its trap?
- Am I afraid of making decisions because I don't want to feel guilty or responsible if the outcome is undesired?

- Do I recognize that when I get stuck in making a decision, it may be the OCD mind influencing me?
- Am I aware of the time I have wasted trying to make the "right" decision?

Getting Stuck in the Search for Certainty

The decisions we make today are based on the information we currently have. Is it fair to later say, "I made the wrong decision" when we don't like the outcome? The judgmental mind will advise: "You should've known better."

Can we instead recognize that if things don't go as we want them to that we can adapt to our circumstances? Most importantly, can we recognize the growth and learning that happens in situations we don't ask for or expect? Though the human mind insists we can control the future, we cannot.

Life would be bliss if our decisions always led to the results we wanted. Unfortunately, this is impossible, unrealistic, and unfair. The human mind cannot predict an outcome. No one knows the future.

Accepting Uncertainty with Faith

Some people say, "the Creator is all-knowing and will tell me what I need to do." Does that mean the Creator has to make sure you get the outcome you'd like every time so you can be free of challenges? It does not.

Life is about uncertainty. If God wanted us to have certainty, God would take us by the hand to ensure we didn't make any mistakes. But that doesn't happen, does it? God allows us to fall so we can learn to pick ourselves up, right?

If our decisions always yielded the right outcome, what would we learn? It takes faith to accept uncertainty and know that turbulent waters are for our good, doesn't it? As we continue to strengthen our faith, we can connect to Deity amid uncertainty.

Find Faith and Put Down Your Sword

In ancient times, warriors often used their swords for worldly prowess, but there were those who realized they didn't have to use weapons. They found something of higher value than fighting physically for their lands and property: their faith in God. Some even buried their weapons.

What about you? You no longer have to fight the scrupulous mind and the internal events that come with it as part of the obsessive-compulsive disorder. The fight is over. Every time your instinct to fight shows up, drop your sword and lift yourself with courage and trust!

When questions such as "Am I worthy of God's love?" show up, consider asking yourself, "Am I willing to have God's love? Am I willing to walk in faith?" Confidently allow any painful internal experiences to naturally come and go without giving in to private or public compulsions!

Invitation

Every day, notice if you are willing to embrace your faith and own your decisions. Become aware of your willingness to take what life offers. Notice if you are using your faith along with the psychological-flexibility skills to keep moving toward a rich and meaningful life despite uncertainty.

The scrupulous mind may try to dissuade you from taking risks and insist you can find all the right answers. It may also say that you have to be perfectly good. After all, it tells you that your relationship with God and your morals are at stake. But compulsions won't get you closer to the stuff you value. You can focus your time and energy on doing what matters most.

The Voices Within

Ron's Story

Ron's thoughts often led to extreme anxiety and uncertainty. He often wondered if these tormenting thoughts meant he was possessed by an evil spirit. "Why else would they keep intruding in my life?" he would often ask his therapist. "Are you sure this is OCD? It sure feels like it is an evil spirit!"

Jen's Story

When Jen read her spiritual books, a thought to reread whatever she was reading would show up. Since she believed the thought was from a Higher Power, she would reread the lines whenever the thought came. Sometimes a thought about sharing her beliefs with others showed up and if she didn't immediately do what her mind was telling her, she felt guilty because she believed she had been disobedient.

According to Jen's and Ron's religious beliefs, the voices within were either from a bad spirit or from a Higher Power. These two didn't realize there was a voice within—the mind. The scrupulous mind was wreaking havoc. The next section will enhance your understanding regarding choices.

You Have Options!

The Language Machine—Review

The amazing language machine's (the mind) main function is to help us survive in the world. The mind produces thoughts day and night, and there are helpful thoughts we need to listen to because they can lead us to what matters most to us.

Are your behaviors done for the sake of relieving anxiety, or are they helping you connect with your values? Whenever you begin to obsess, it's most likely the scrupulous mind.

Whenever your mind provides advice, ask yourself this question:

> "If I act on this advice, will it truly get me closer to who I want to be and what matters most to me?"

- When you cannot do anything about the mind's advice and it's causing you distress,
  - Acknowledge your internal events and defuse accordingly ("I hear you. You may be right. Thanks, Mind. We'll see what happens.").
  - Allow the internal events (e.g., "Hello, old friend.").
  - Then gently refocus on what you were doing.
- Whenever your mind provides advice, you act on the internal event (i.e., thought or feeling), and discover that your actions are taking you away from what matters most in that moment (because you got stuck in the scrupulosity trap),
  - Acknowledge the internal events ("I just got hooked.").
  - Allow the discomfort ("I can breathe in and out to create space for anxiety.").
  - Then gently come back to the present moment and keep moving toward your values.

- When you cannot act on the advice in the moment, and if you did, it would take you closer to your values,
    - Make a note to act on it later.
    - Then come back to the present moment—the moment that matters most.
- Whenever your mind provides advice, you act on the advice, and your actions take you closer to who you want to be and what matters most, carry on!

> When you face unpleasant external and internal experiences, what path will you choose? Willingness skills can help you choose the path that gets you closer to your values, even when it's the harder path.

Choose the Path Less Traveled

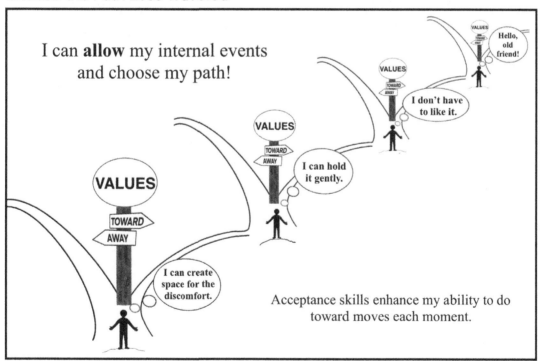

Use your values (e.g., connecting with Deity) to help you live the way you'd like to because they are your guide no matter how turbulent the waters may feel as you journey through life.

> Remember: Your choice to live your values is ongoing.

Invitation

- What actions will help me do what matters most in the life domains I've neglected?

- What skills will I implement when the preachy mind brings up unnecessary rules that get in the way of my faith and other values?

> You can discover that you can be imperfectly good and experience inner strength and satisfaction despite unpleasant internal events.

9

Connecting to the Present Moment

We should wisely live a day at a time because that is all we have.

—*Marvin J. Ashton*

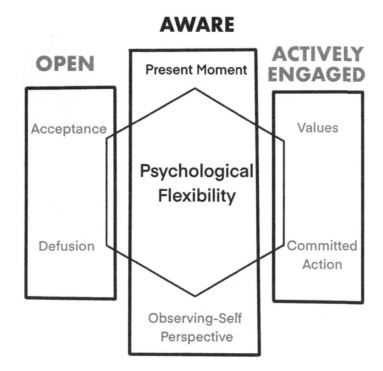

Joe's Story

Whenever Joe heard the words service, kindness, and charity while at work, he'd ask himself, "Am I doing enough? Am I doing the right things? Am I impacting people's lives?" And he would spiral into the scrupulosity trap. He would try to remember past experiences and question his intentions. And try as he might, his attention would drift all afternoon. He didn't know how to acknowledge his internal experiences and gently shift his attention back to the present moment.

The human mind continually produces thoughts. Some of us have more active minds than others. It is how we respond to these thoughts that really matters (e.g., Joe usually got hooked with his thoughts and feelings). This chapter provides several ways you can learn to connect back to the present moment when your attention drifts elsewhere (i.e., past or future).

Please remember that learning to connect to the present moment is a process.

Where Is Your Focus?

This illustration may be familiar to you, especially if you took Psychology 101 in college. Do you see two images? Take a break if you can't see both right away, then come back.

Now, can you see both images, and if you do, can you see both at the exact same time?

It may seem like you can see a young woman and an elderly woman at the same time, but it actually requires a few microseconds for your attention to shift from one to the other. Sometimes we think we can focus on two or more things at the same time, but is that really so, and why is it important to discuss this?

Your Brain Can Only Focus on One Thing at a Time

As you read these lines, you are not only reading but thinking about what you are reading. And something you read may trigger thoughts about something else. You may also notice bodily sensations, like hunger and pain. You may hear the sound of a siren and suddenly feel anxious. Then you may hear dogs barking outside and get distracted by another thought and so on.

When you are "multitasking,"[1] you are actually switching between tasks at hyperspeed and making your brain work harder than it needs to, even if it's only for microseconds. There can be several things going on around you and inside you in the here and now, but there are always those microseconds between each of those events.

Choosing What to Focus On

Although all those internal and external events are occurring at the same time, you get to choose what to focus on. Focusing on your difficult internal experiences, such as intrusive thoughts related to scrupulosity OCD, is the easy, though not the best, option. The good news is that you can also choose to focus on your senses (e.g., what you see, hear, smell, touch, or taste) even when uncomfortable internal experiences are present.

For example, paying attention to one of your senses (e.g., noticing three objects that you see and describing them in detail) is not going to get rid of the distressing internal events, but it will dim them just a little so that you can allow them to take their course naturally instead of trying to get rid of them and getting stuck in the scrupulosity trap.

Fears about the Present Moment

Like many, you may be scared to pay attention to the present moment. It may feel impossible. This is normal as this is a new experience. Few are those who can naturally notice their attention drifting and softly bring it back to what is going on in the present. Lucky them! Most people's minds are constantly drifting, and that's okay.

I will share several exercises to help you connect to the present moment. Try them one at a time at your own pace, slowly working through all of them. Find the ones that you like and that make sense to you. These exercises will enhance your mental flexibility.

> The natural mind is a wandering mind.
> You are learning how to respond to it.
> Slow and steady wins the race!

Exercise 1. Anchoring on Your Breath

> *Breathing is like an anchor in the midst of an emotional storm: the anchor won't get rid of the storm, but it will hold you steady until it passes.*
>
> —Russ Harris[2]

Ships in a harbor need to be anchored when they are brought back in from a day at sea. If not secured, they will drift away, especially if a storm comes in during the night. Like a ship in the harbor anchors to stay safe, you can anchor during scrupulosity storms.

- Take a minute or two every day, or as often as you remember, to practice anchoring on your breath.

- You can close your eyes or focus on an object as you practice.

- Notice your breathing. You don't need to purposely inhale or exhale deeply. Just notice the way you are breathing. You may want to notice the temperature of the air coming in and out or the way your chest or stomach rises and falls.

- Notice how quickly your mind begins to distract you. Acknowledge the mind ("There goes my mind again!") and gently anchor back on your breathing.

- Continue noticing your breathing and acknowledging the mind.

This brief exercise will enable you to enhance your awareness so that whenever difficult experiences show up, you can choose how to respond to them and gently anchor on the present moment—not necessarily on your breathing but on the activities you value in life.

As you do this and the other exercises in this workbook, you may feel relaxed and relieved after connecting to the present moment. That's okay, but remember, that's not the goal. The goal is to develop psychological flexibility.

> Anchoring on your breath allows you to be open to
> what is in the moment without reacting to the scrupulous mind.

Exercise 2. "Cubbyholing"[3]

Where Does the Internal Experience Belong?

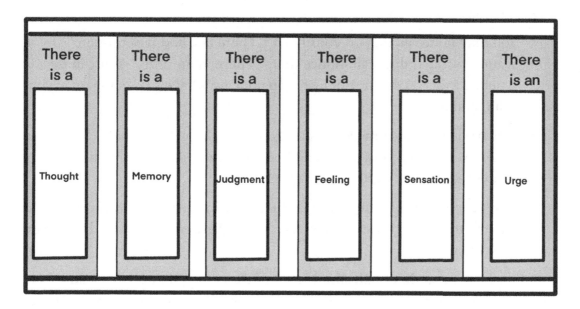

You may remember that when you were in kindergarten, each kid in the classroom had a cubbyhole in which to place their belongings. In this exercise, you will learn to notice your internal events, place them in their own cubbyholes, and acknowledge them instead of getting caught up in the content of each internal experience.

You may want to write the names of each cubbyhole on a sticky note before beginning the exercise or take a photo of the graphic above.

Set your alarm for three minutes the first time you do this exercise. Then do it again for five. As you practice, your awareness and ability to acknowledge your internal experiences will increase and you will be able to do what matters each day.

- Sit quietly and notice the internal events occurring inside your mind and body. Acknowledge them one at a time. For example, you may notice the thought "I'm not sure about this practice." Identify it. "**There is a** thought." Another thought may show up. "I don't think I understand this practice." Acknowledge it again. "**There is a** thought."

- You may notice your mind going blank. Notice what happens afterward. "I cannot think of anything. My mind has gone blank." Recognize it. "**There is a** thought!"

- You may get frustrated. Notice it. "**There is a** feeling."

- You may notice an itch on your head. "**There is a** bodily sensation." If you want to scratch that itch, notice that. "**There is an** urge." You can decide whether to act on the urge or just keep noticing what else is going on in your mind and body.

- When you have the urge to purposely think, acknowledge that. "There is an urge." Remember, your mind and body are always doing something. There is no need to force anything to happen.

- The purpose of this exercise is to help you increase your awareness and expand the space that exists between internal experiences and what you do with them.

- It's best if you **don't take shortcuts** by just saying "thought," "feeling," etc. You are becoming an observer of your internal events; thus, saying, "**There is a** _____" is best while doing this practice.

See if you can do it again for five more minutes and more regularly. Be curious and notice how fast your mind works! Practice cubbyholing as often as you'd like. Note what you've learned after practicing this exercise several times.

Between stimulus and response there is a space. In that space is our power to choose our response. In our response lies our growth and our freedom.

—*Viktor E. Frankl*[4]

Exercise 3. Mindful Eating

In many cultures, eating is an event where people gather to enjoy food and connect. In other cultures, eating is something people do on the run as they believe there is never enough time to get everything done.

Many people try to catch up with the news, their email, or other tasks while they eat. Then there are those who are not in a hurry and leisurely eat their meals while watching TV or catching up on their social media feeds. Many of us simply don't take time to be in the present with our food—to be grateful for it and enjoy it fully.

Studies[5] confirm that there is a significant connection between the gut and the nervous system. In fact, it takes about twenty minutes after eating for the brain to register the signal of being full. When you eat quickly and/or while doing other things, your brain may not recognize the signal of satiety, and you may end up eating more than you need to.

These studies also indicate that digestion can slow down or stop when we are distracted by other activities, such as driving or typing on a computer. This also occurs when we experience the fight-or-flight response. If we are not able to digest well, both our physical and mental health suffer.

Because we need to eat, mindful eating can be an effective way to help us connect with the present moment every day. And, of course, your digestive system will thank you as you mindfully enjoy your food.

Noticing Your Eating

Make a conscious decision to eat mindfully for at least the first few bites of each meal. As you develop this habit, it will become second nature, and you can then increase the time you eat mindfully.

- Start by noticing the color and variety of the food in front of you.
- Notice and acknowledge what your mind says and defuse as needed.

- Think about what it took to get this food in front of you.
  - How many people besides you were involved in making this moment possible? Take a moment to think about this and feel gratitude.
- Before you take your first bite, bring it toward you so you can smell it.
- Take the stance of curiosity, as if you've never tasted this food before. Close your eyes and imagine it being a delicacy. Savor the moment as you smell it. Then bring it to your mouth.
- Take a bite and begin to chew slowly.
- As you chew, notice the flavor and texture of the food, alternating your focus.
- Savor the bite for at least thirty seconds and keep noticing the flavor, texture, and even the sound as you chew.
- Can you do all these things before swallowing? See whether you can delay swallowing your food for at least five more seconds.
- Next, notice what the mind is saying. Acknowledge and defuse as usual, then reconnect with your food.
- Notice how your body feels after taking that first bite. You may notice the urge to stop eating mindfully. You may notice the urge to eat faster. Acknowledge that and defuse. ("I'm noticing my hunger." "I'm noticing the thought that I don't want to do this!" "Thanks, Mind!")

Now you are ready to take your second bite. You may have the urge to take bigger bites and eat fast. Remember, you don't need to do everything your mind tells you to.

You can decide to eat mindfully instead of engaging in activities that interrupt your digestion.

Mindful eating is an almost effortless way to enhance your awareness. Try it at least once a day and notice the difference it makes whenever scrupulosity storms come upon you.

Exercise 4. Mindful Walking

The ability to walk is a gift we often take for granted. A handy and effortless way to increase your awareness is by connecting with the present when walking.

Whenever you walk, you can choose to problem-solve, daydream, obsess, stress—and forget to connect with the present.

You can make an effort to be mindful at least once a day as you're walking to your car, the grocery store, a classroom, the doctor's office, etc. Or maybe you want to be mindful so you can prepare for a specific situation, like a job interview, presentation, or special date. Go for a walk before the event and follow the instructions below.

Noticing Your External World

- As you begin your walk, become aware of your surroundings by using at least three senses (e.g., sight, sound, and touch).

- Notice what you see, hear, and feel in your body as you walk. Observe with curiosity any objects you may come across and acknowledge your mind when it starts chattering as usual. ("Thanks, Mind.") Then go back to noticing.

- Notice objects that may be part of nature as well as things that are manmade. For example, you may say to yourself, "I'm noticing how large the leaves on that tree are. The leaves are dark, and some branches are losing their leaves" or "I am noticing it is quiet in this area of the parking lot." Don't worry when your attention drifts. Acknowledge it and gently go back to noticing.

- At some point, you may get hooked. "That person's clothing is so tight! Oh, shoot. Did I just lust?" When you recognize you've become hooked, acknowledge the thoughts, feelings, and other internal events. ("I'm noticing the thought that I may have lusted." "I'm noticing the sensation of tightness in my chest.") Then gently go back to noticing your surroundings.

- Keep acknowledging what you notice with your senses and getting unhooked as needed.

Alternate between noticing the external world with your senses and noticing what your body is doing and how it feels as you walk. And, of course, be aware of when the mind begins to put in its two cents, and act accordingly. Have fun walking mindfully!

Exercise 5. Daily Tasks and Your Five Senses

As you go about your daily tasks, you can use your senses to help you anchor in the present moment. For example:

- Brush your teeth and use your five senses one at a time. Notice when your attention goes elsewhere, gently acknowledge it, and bring it back to the taste of your toothpaste or the sound you are making as you brush.

- As you are working or doing any other activity, become aware of your attention drifting and acknowledge it ("I'm noticing my worry thoughts about my donation yesterday. Was it enough? I hear you, Mind. Thanks!"), then go back to your task.

- When you are waiting to pay at a store, can you notice the sounds around you and notice that you are noticing?

- Whenever you have to stop at a red light, breathe in deeply, exhale slowly, and scan your body from head to toe. Continue noticing your breathing and what your body is doing until the light turns green.

Make a conscious effort for one or two minutes to notice being in the present moment by anchoring on any of your senses. When your mind distracts you, gently bring your attention back.

> Practice makes for progress and change!

Ethan's Story

Ethan had been practicing the new flexibility skills he was learning, but one day, he said, "I got totally hooked the other day. What should I do so I don't get stuck?" His therapist clarified his situation to ensure he wasn't trying to find a way to get relief from his anxiety, then shared the following practice.

Exercise 6. Getting Back to BASE

You can get back to BASE right here, right now, instead of getting stuck (behaving compulsively) shoveling deeper into the scrupulosity trap.

- **B**reathe in slowly and notice the way you are breathing for a few moments. When you exhale, try to do so slowly. Continue noticing your breathing.
- **A**cknowledge your thoughts and feelings (e.g., I'm noticing the thought that I may have cheated on my test. I am noticing anxiety and uncertainty.)
- **S**can your body and notice any sensations there. Connect with your body by noticing the temperature of your skin in different parts of your body. If possible, touch your face, hands, arms, and feet. How hot, warm, or cold do they feel? Acknowledge that. ("I'm noticing my hands are cold. I'm noticing my face is hot.")
- **E**ngage in what matters right now. What is it you were doing before being hooked by your mind? Gently shift your focus back to that activity right here, right now. Repeat connecting back to BASE for a few more moments.

Applying BASE skills during calm times can enhance your understanding of how to apply them effectively when you find yourself caught up in a scrupulosity storm.

The verses of this prayer (an alternative to Reinhold Niebuhr's Serenity Prayer) are relevant as we learn to let go of the struggles and accept what is in the moment.

> Let me give my permission (accept) for life to be as I find it (as life is, was, or may be) even though I may not approve of what I find.
>
> I have wisdom to see what would be good to change, willingness to act, willingness to follow through, and the gratitude for the opportunity to try to live my life as best I can.
>
> —*Hank Robb*[6]

Invitation

Notice how often you want to control your internal experiences and other people's actions. You can decide to be willing to take what's being offered and have the courage to face what is presented, right here, right now.

10

Being Aware of Being Aware

Whatever you are thinking, whatever you are feeling, whatever you're sensing, whatever you're doing, this part of you is always there, aware of it.

—*Steven C. Hayes*

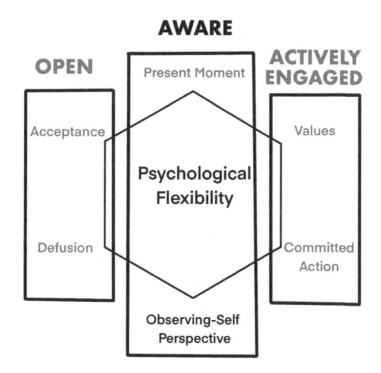

The Thinking Part of Us versus the Observing Part of Us

Whenever we are in a problem-solving mode or precarious situation, our mind comes to the rescue, and that's when we automatically access the thinking part of us. Accessing our thinking-self mode can be helpful when we are problem-solving, working, studying, creating, imagining, analyzing, remembering, and visualizing, among the many other helpful activities we engage in daily. But sometimes the amazing mind gets carried away and produces thoughts that limit us. Whenever you obsess about the past or worry about the future, you are in the thinking-self mode.

When the thinking-self mode is in the limelight, the observing-self mode fades to the background.

An excellent example of how our observing-self viewpoint gets overshadowed by our thinking-self perspective is when we are traveling—you know, those moments when people are at a crowded tourist site, taking *selfies* to show family and friends the awesome places they have visited? Ironically, they may not have taken the time to truly enjoy the site by just observing, being present, and using their senses to take it all in.

Instead, they frantically took pictures they could show their friends. Later that evening, as they downloaded their photos to email or post them, they realized they hadn't enjoyed the experience. They'd been too focused on the task and hadn't savored the moment.

Another example of how often we can shift our perspective is when we witness a beautiful sunset. We may feel grateful for the beautiful world. Right then, we may be accessing the observing-self mode. But soon the problem-solving mind starts talking. "Mom would love to see this amazing sunset. Where is my smartphone?" We start looking for our phone so we can take pictures, and we end up missing the beautiful sunset.

We began with the observing-self perspective, but within microseconds, our perspective shifted to the thinking-self perspective because we tried to think and problem-solve (finding our smartphone to take a photo).

It happens. It's human nature. However, when we experience psychological **inflexibility**, we tend to get stuck in the thinking, problem-solving mindset.

When this happens, we can become fused or hooked with our internal events and see ourselves in a negative light. We may be unwilling to embrace difficulties.

We may find ourselves stuck in the past or future, lacking clarity about what we value and unable to act on what matters most in our lives.

Understanding the difference between both perspectives can be confusing for some. Let's briefly clarify.

The Thinking-Self Perspective

- This is the part of us that thinks, plans, and solves problems at work, school, home, or in any setting in life. It creates memories, images, evaluations, beliefs, and a myriad of thoughts.

- Our human experience includes trials, flaws, and mistakes. Our thinking self helps us figure things out; however, as discussed earlier, its advice is not always helpful.

- Our thinking self is essential to surviving our earthly journey.

- Your thinking self is in high gear when you get stuck in the scrupulosity trap.

> *It is what makes us human, what distinguishes us from other animals. We can be aware of being aware.*
>
> —*Jon Kabat-Zinn*[1]

The Observing-Self Perspective

This perspective can assist us when we become hooked with unhelpful internal events.

- The observing self allows us to notice what's really going on around and inside of us so we can make wiser decisions regarding what is happening in the moment—either internally or externally.

- It helps us notice what life is really about and see life from a different viewpoint.
- Though we are not our internal experiences, we can respond in helpful ways as we access our observing-self perspective.
- Accessing the observing part of us will enable us to become aware of being aware!

Remember why you do what you do every day (i.e., what matters most to you). Focus on the process. The observing part of you can help you along the way. It's about making progress, not attaining perfection!

> Connecting to the present moment can strengthen your ability to access the observing part of you and help you become flexible whenever scrupulosity storms loom on the horizon.

Spencer's Story

Spencer had experienced anxiety since childhood but didn't know he had scrupulosity OCD until he was in his early twenties. He had placed several labels on himself, such as "I am dishonest," "I'm anxious," "I'm never good enough," and "I'm a failure." He didn't know he didn't need to believe these labels or be those labels until he learned to become flexible with his internal experiences.

Exercise 1. "I Am . . ."[2]

This practice can help you change your view of difficult internal events, just as Spencer did.

- Go ahead complete the following sentences. Just write what shows up in your mind. Don't overthink it.
  I am _____.
  I am _____.
  I am _____.
  I am _____.

  For example: I am *kind*. I am *honest*. I am *an anxious person*. I am *bad*. As you read these sentences (positive or negative), ask yourself, "Am I that way 100 percent of the time whether I am alone or with others?" It may feel like it, but are you really that way all the time, everywhere, with everyone, 24/7? No, you're not.

- Next, erase or cross out the period and add *or not* to each sentence.

  For example: I am kind *or not*. I am honest *or not*. I am an anxious person *or not*. I am bad *or not*.

  How do you feel when you read those new sentences, and what is your mind saying about it? Just notice your thoughts.

- Now, cross out all the words in each sentence except for "I am."

  For example: I am ~~kind or not~~. I am ~~honest or not~~. I am ~~an anxious person or not~~. I am ~~bad or not.~~

  Imagine what life would be like if you weren't attached to those labels. Who are you when you are not stuck with the content of those words? Ponder that.

- Slowly repeat the words "I am" aloud four times. "I am. I am. I am. I am."

- Pay attention to your feelings as you say those words. Have you noticed that you are more than any roles, labels, stories, thoughts, or feelings about yourself? Can you recognize that there are many ways to see yourself? Are you willing to create some flexibility with what your mind is telling you?

- The next time you refer to yourself with a permanent label, recognize that label is related to how you feel or think.

- For example, if you wrote: "I am not kind," acknowledge the thought by saying, "I'm noticing I'm having the thought that I'm not kind." (see page 80) Do you see the difference?

- When you feel anxious, instead of labeling yourself with "I am an anxious person," you can acknowledge that it's just a feeling. "I'm noticing I'm having the feeling of anxiety when I go to social gatherings."
- When a thought like, "I am bad" shows up, you can acknowledge the thought, "I'm noticing I'm having the thought that I'm bad."

Notice how the labels others or your mind have stamped on you are influencing your everyday living. Can you recognize that it is impossible for anyone to be a particular way 100 percent of the time, 24/7, each minute of their lives whether they are alone or with others?

Acknowledging that those labels are related to thoughts and feelings and other internal experiences (e.g., evaluations, memories, sensations) can enhance your ability to choose how to respond to what others or your mind say about you. None of us needs to be ruled by any labels any longer. Most importantly, we don't need to let them get in the way of our living a vibrant, meaningful life.

> The labels we assign ourselves do not determine who we are.
> Our internal experiences change according to the circumstances
> in which we find ourselves at any given moment.

Lauren's Story

Lauren felt hopeless. She was doing everything she could to be a good mom, but the scrupulous mind always seemed to find a way to get her digging back into the scrupulosity trap. "What if my fears come true? I won't be able to live with myself if I end up hurting my children. I'd rather die." She had great difficulty recognizing that she was not her thoughts and that her thoughts were **not external behaviors**.

You may feel like Lauren. But you are not alone on this hard journey. Give the following exercise a try and see what you learn.

Exercise 2. The Visitor's Message[3]

Read the instructions several times or record them on your smartphone so you can do this exercise as often as you'd like.

- Sit comfortably and notice how your body feels where you are seated.
- Notice your feet on the ground in this moment. Slowly become aware of your legs and the rest of your body, all the way up to your abdomen. Feel your back against the chair or couch. Notice how your back feels next to the clothes you are wearing.
- Pay attention to the temperature of the room by noticing your hands, arms, and face. Notice when your mind starts sharing its opinions. Acknowledge that and defuse as needed.
- Now, imagine someone standing just a few feet from you. This person is visiting you in this moment and looking at you with compassion. This person wants to help you and knows your thoughts, feelings, and sensations.
- The only difference between you and this visitor is that this person is you, only twenty years older. Your older self understands your pain, struggles, intentions, and dreams and has become wiser over time.
- If this visitor could give you some advice to help you with the pain and suffering you are experiencing related to your scrupulosity OCD, what would it be?
- Imagine your "wiser self" taking a piece of paper and condensing that advice into one sentence. Your wiser self wants you to have this message, so it places it on your lap and walks away.
- For a few minutes, imagine reading the message and pondering the advice your wiser self has given you regarding the pain you experience because of scrupulosity OCD.
- Start noticing your body and where you are sitting. Feel your body against the chair or couch. Notice where your feet are and the way you are breathing.
- Take a deep breath and exhale slowly. Take a few more deep breaths, and when you are ready, open your eyes. Then notice your body temperature by touching your hands, and be aware of where you are right now.

Go ahead and write the message, then ponder the advice the wiser part of you wants you to act on. Decide what actions you'll take regarding this message.

> It's human nature to place undue pressure on ourselves.
> If you struggle with scrupulosity OCD, take time to think about what your wiser self might say to you when you are struggling.

11

Developing Self-Forgiveness and Self-Compassion

Forgiveness is for yourself because it frees you. It lets you out of that prison you put yourself in.

—Louise Hay

Mary's Story

Mary's marriage ended in divorce after two years. She'd often say, "Before the wedding, I had a foreboding that I shouldn't marry him. It was the voice of God, and I didn't listen. It's all my fault." Guilt had taken over her life.

The Scrupulous Mind and the Blame Trap[1]

The scrupulous mind can easily get you stuck in the blame trap. It may tell you that you are responsible—even when you aren't. In Mary's case, the voice may have been from God, but did she need to continue to blame herself for her ex-husband's choices?

What is your default reaction when you experience guilt and/or a high sense of responsibility? Is the scrupulous mind leading you to believe you have to do more and more? "What will you do when nothing you do will do?"[2]

When you ruminate or obsess about all the possible situations whether you are or aren't responsible and you blame yourself (or others), how motivated and empowered do you feel?

Notice the examples in the chart below. What statements do you use when you blame yourself, and how empowered (or not) do you feel as a result? You may say,

"I already know it's not helpful," but I invite you to do this practice to enhance your awareness.

Self-Blame Tracking

Blaming Statements	Empowerment Felt (1–10, with 10 = feeling empowered)
"I should've been stronger."	2
"I'm a terrible parent!"	1

Response-Ability

We all need to take responsibility for our actions. But when we are fused with difficult thoughts because the scrupulous mind tells us we're responsible for things we cannot control (e.g., illness, accidents, inexperience, etc.) or have already taken care of, it's best to have "response-ability." **This means we develop the ability to respond differently to our internal and external events.**

Every time your mind takes you to the blame trap, acknowledge it and use a defusion skill. "I hear you. You're good at this, Mind! I'm noticing the feeling of guilt." Then gently get back to what matters in the present moment.

> *What's most important may not be what you do, but what you do after what you did!*
>
> —*Garry Landreth*[3]

Exercise 1. Naming Your Story

We all have a story that repeats itself, a story that may end up haunting us. (Please see note on page 52). For example, Mary blamed herself for her divorce, but once she learned psychological-flexibility skills and the old story showed up, she could respond with, "There is the *premonition* story. You're good at bringing up that story, Mind." Then she would gently shift her attention back to what mattered right then and there instead of digging herself into the blame trap. Whenever the thought came back, she would acknowledge it and gently come back to the present moment. You can also name your story.

1. Think about when your story began.
2. Notice how often the story repeats itself and hooks you.
3. Give it a name related to the situation or how you feel when it shows up. When you notice you have become fused with it, acknowledge it by saying something like, "Of course, there is the (name of your story). I'm not surprised."
4. Make sure you do not name the story with words that are negative or judgmental of you or others. Just use a name related to the story.
5. Gently bring yourself back to the present moment—to what matters most in that moment and in your life.

You may have more than one story. Name them and acknowledge them for what they are: memories and stories that may be getting in the way of you living your life. You can connect to the here and now instead of being caught up in a memory or story.

Noticing How You Treat Yourself

"The greatest trap in our life is not success, popularity or power, but self-rejection."

—Henri Nouwen[4]

Ponder Your Answers to the Following Questions

- If you have no confidence in yourself and nothing left to offer, can you really love and serve those around you?
- Does self-loathing make you a better person?
- Do you believe you need to sacrifice loving yourself? If so, why?
- When you don't appreciate who you are, does it help you in any way?
- Can you give what you don't have?

It's so much easier to forgive others than to forgive ourselves. Do you have a difficult time forgiving yourself for past mistakes? Is your mind saying you have not done enough to be forgiven by God and/or others and thus you cannot forgive yourself? Maybe you never did anything wrong, yet remorse, shame, and guilt are your companions. Does it help when you begin to obsess and give in to compulsions?

You don't have to listen to the unhelpful voices in the world or within you. The following exercise will help you increase your awareness and be able to choose whether to act on the voices you hear within and without.

Exercise 2. Letting Your Younger Self Speak[5]

- Find a comfortable, quiet place to practice.
- Now, think of when you were a young child. Can you go back in time and see yourself as young as you can remember? Maybe you were five or six years old. Imagine yourself at that age in your favorite outfit, shirt, hat, or shoes. Try to remember what your hair and face looked like and how tall you were.
- Try to get a clear picture of yourself as a young child. Imagine that child saying the same words you say to yourself when you beat yourself up. How do you feel as you hear those words coming out of that child in the voice of that child?
- Hear your younger self say those words again. Notice how your mind and body respond to that young child's self-critical statements. As you hear

these words, notice any feelings of compassion and kindness that arise toward this child.

- What would you tell this young child as you hear him/her say those mean words to herself/himself?

- For a moment, notice the feelings you are experiencing toward this child (you). Take a few more moments to notice those feelings.

When you notice you're becoming hooked by evaluative thoughts, remember this young child saying those words. Can you develop kindness and compassion for your present self as you would for that young child?

To help you develop self-forgiveness and self-compassion, try listening in the voice of that child when you notice yourself falling into the judgment trap.

Exercise 3. Treating Shame as You Would a Friend Who Is Ill[6]

Though the scrupulous mind insists that you need to surrender or get rid of your painful internal experiences like shame, you can learn to respond differently. You can recognize that shame is a natural feeling that shows up when you get caught in the content of your thoughts and memories.

Read the instructions for the following exercise all the way through or record them on your smartphone if you'd prefer, so you can listen to them as often as you'd like.

- Sit comfortably and close your eyes. Imagine a situation that brings you shame. As you do, imagine treating this feeling as you would a dear friend who is ill.

- If your friend were talking about their illness, would you pay attention to them, even if you didn't want to and it made you uncomfortable? Notice the feeling and listen to what shame is saying, just as you would listen to a friend.

- Even if you were tired, you would still honor your friend by listening politely and empathetically. Notice when the scrupulous mind starts giving you unhelpful advice. Acknowledge it. "I'm noticing I'm having the thought that I am sinful." "I'm noticing the feeling of shame taking over my body."

- Then gently notice the emotion with compassion, just as you would feel compassion for a friend who is ill.

- Take a few more moments to imagine looking at shame and embracing it with curiosity, like you would a friend who wants to share their struggles.

- Notice what it's like to have compassion toward shame. If your mind starts talking, gently acknowledge, defuse, and return to noticing the feeling with compassion.

Remember that emotions are part of the human experience. When shame is present, honor it in that moment.

After doing this practice at least three times, jot down your insights and what you've learned.

Exercise 4. Contemplating Guilt as You Would a Fascinating Painting[7]

Guilt is a feeling that can help us make amends when we've done something wrong. However, individuals struggling with scrupulosity OCD tend to feel hyper-responsible for situations that are/were not in their control.

Read the instructions for the following exercise or record them on your smartphone.

Close your eyes and imagine looking at your painful emotion or the bodily sensation related to that emotion as you would a fascinating painting. See guilt as if it were a piece of art you are contemplating. Notice its colors, shapes, and how it is presented right there in front of you. Take a few moments to contemplate guilt.

Continue to observe it and keep an eye on the mind. Unhook from any unhelpful thoughts, feelings, or other internal events as needed by acknowledging them.

Embrace the painting—e.g., the guilt—for a few more moments. When ready, gently shift your attention back to the present moment.

After doing this exercise several times, write about your insights. What did you learn? And if you like this practice, you can do it with other emotions as well.

Invitation

Whenever you begin to beat yourself up as if you deserve punishment because you may be hooked with thoughts such as "It was my fault" and "I know better," remember, **you hurt where you care.**[8]

Developing Self-Compassion

"If your compassion does not include yourself, it is incomplete"

—Jack Kornfield[9]

Research shows that when people are self-compassionate, they recognize hardships as part of life and ruminate less on how things should be. Self-compassionate people see life from a perspective that helps improve their mental health. Self-compassion increases inner strength, courage, and resilience in the face of difficult situations. Self-compassionate people are more caring and supportive in their relationships.[10]

Some people worry that in loving themselves they're being selfish and, worse, narcissistic. The reality is that the scrupulous mind is leading you to become the extreme opposite of a narcissist. As you get fused with unhelpful thoughts and feelings, you begin to feel miserable and fail to give yourself even a crumb of love. Is that working out for you? Would God want you to mistreat yourself? You can develop self-compassion skills. Let's talk about how you can begin.

Implementing the following three[11] principles can help you develop self-compassion:

1. Connect to the present moment of pain
2. Remember your common humanity with others
3. Show loving-kindness to yourself in difficult times

In a conversation I had with Reverend Katie O'Dunne on October 12, 2022, she shared how she invites her clients to add a spiritual component to their self-compassion skills. Reverend O'Dunne serves clients of all faiths who struggle with scrupulosity and other OCD themes. I would also like to invite you to include God and faith as you continue to develop self-compassion.

If moral scrupulosity is your challenge, I invite you to remember your values—what makes your heart sing and whole insides leap—as you continue to build your self-compassion.

Experiencing scrupulosity OCD is an intense hardship. You need and deserve to treat yourself with kindness. Just as you care for others, you can care for yourself, especially when you get stuck in the scrupulosity trap. Let's dive a little deeper into these three-principles.

1. In the Moment of Pain, Connect to the Present Moment

Take a minute to think of a loved one who has experienced a failure, feels inadequate, or may be struggling with a challenge similar to yours.

- In the moment of pain, what would you say to acknowledge their feelings? ("I know you don't like feeling this way. Shame hurts a lot.") Go ahead and write your answer.

- Take a moment and think of your suffering. Imagine your loved one telling you these words.

- Now, change the statement for yourself. ("I don't like feeling this way. Shame hurts a lot!")

When others suffer, you don't blame them for their flaws or misdoings. You love and feel empathy for them. When you become fused with the content of your thoughts ("I should be doing more for others!"), treat yourself as you would a loved one.

Examples of statements to connect to the present moment and acknowledge your pain follow:

- "I'm having a hard time with guilt right now."
- "My blasphemous thoughts are painful. God is aware of my affliction."
- "Here is the 'tax story.' I'll let it be there for now."

2. Common Humanity

Think about your loved one again.

- What could you say to acknowledge that they are not alone in their suffering? Would you refer to their faith and invite them to remember God? ("You are not alone. I'm here for you. God knows your suffering.")

- Take a moment to imagine your loved one saying these same words to you during a difficult time.

- Now, write the same statement as if you were saying it to yourself. ("I'm not alone. God knows my suffering.")

Remembering that you are not alone can help during painful moments. There are many who suffer from obsessive-compulsive disorder, and everyone experiences struggles of one kind or another. When you experience sorrow, loneliness, anxiety, uncertainty, and other unpleasant emotions, remember that you are not alone!

Sample statements to remember you are not alone:

- "Pain is part of life, and God is aware of everyone's challenges."

- "There are others experiencing similar emotions."

- "Others also doubt their character. Like others, I can choose to focus on what matters."

3. Loving-Kindness

Take another moment to think of a loved one who might be struggling with a challenge similar to yours.

- What might they need to hear in that moment of pain? ("May you be patient and hopeful.") Do they need to have more courage, patience, endurance, forgiveness, resilience, and/or hope in addition to kindness and compassion during hard times?

- Take a few seconds to think of your suffering and imagine your loved one saying those kind words to you.

- Now, write that same statement for yourself. ("I can be patient and hopeful.")

It's easy to be kind with our loved ones but harder to be kind with ourselves. If we develop self-kindness and self-compassion, we'll have enough love to share with others.

Loving-kindness statements:

- "I can forgive myself and remember God's unconditional love."

- "God is kind. I can also be kind with myself."

- "I can keep hoping as I focus on being loving."

The Love Hormone

When we connect with other human beings physically and emotionally, oxytocin, commonly known as the "love hormone," is released.

When we see a loved one suffer, we wish we could take their pain away. We show compassion with kind gestures, such as hugs or handholding. These types of gestures can make a big difference. But when it comes to showing loving-kindness to ourselves, what can we do?

Think about your loved one again.

- What kind gestures, such as hugs, handholding, or soft touches (e.g., a pat on the arm or shoulder) would you share with your loved one in their moment of pain?

- Pause for a moment and think of your struggles. Imagine your loved one offering that same physical gesture to you.

- What kind gesture will you show yourself when you feel overwhelmed by your pain? You could place your hand on your heart as you repeat a self-compassion mantra.

Self-Compassion Mantra

There will be times when you need comfort and no one is there. The good news is that you can embrace yourself[12] with a kind gesture as you repeat your self-compassion mantra to release oxytocin during difficult times.

Your self-compassion mantra can be the statements you wrote for each principle. You can also write a general statement you adjust to different circumstances. Add God and/or your values if you'd like. Do what feels right for you.

For example:

> I don't like shame. It hurts a lot!
> I'm not alone, and God knows my suffering.
> I can be patient and hopeful.

Write your self-compassion mantra here and indicate the gesture you'll use to show loving-kindness to yourself:

You may want to write it on your smartphone or a sticky note so you can remember to be kind to yourself every day. Showing acts of kindness to yourself allows oxytocin to be released, which leaves you feeling more loved, supported, patient, motivated, strengthened, and validated in moments of suffering.

Please don't confuse self-compassion statements with positive self-affirmations. They are **not** the same. Self-compassion statements help you **acknowledge the pain in the moment, recognize it is universal, and recall that you are not alone.** It helps you remember that others care about you and that God is aware of your pain and loves you unconditionally despite what the scrupulous mind says!

You'll find that when you are kind to yourself, you're actually kinder to others. There is plenty of research that shows this to be true. Find out for yourself!

Scrupulosity OCD may be keeping you from living up to your potential. As the fog dissipates, fear can ensue. The following quote can inspire you to not only have self-compassion but to know you don't need to fear who you can become.

> Our deepest fear is not that we are inadequate. Our deepest fear is that we are powerful beyond measure. It is our light, not our darkness that most frightens us. We ask ourselves, "Who am I to be brilliant, gorgeous, talented, fabulous?" Actually, who are you not to be? You are a child of God. Your

playing small does not serve the world. There is nothing enlightened about shrinking so that other people won't feel insecure around you. We are all meant to shine, as children do. We were born to make manifest the glory of God that is within us. It's not just in some of us; it's in everyone. And as we let our own light shine, we unconsciously give other people permission to do the same. As we are liberated from our own fear, our presence automatically liberates others.

—*Marianne Williamson*[13]

Invitation

As you go about life, note how you treat yourself. Self-compassion and self-forgiveness are essential for everyone. Focus on the process. In practicing self-compassion, you can become your own best friend and remember that others and God care about you during hard times.

> Act instead of being acted upon by the scrupulous mind.

12

Staying on the Path Less Traveled

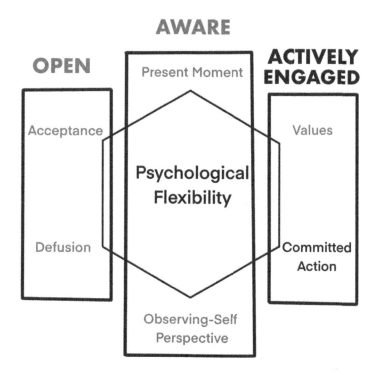

The Stones in Your Vessel of Light[1]

Imagine that when you were born, you entered mortality with a vessel of light—a radiant light emanating love, confidence, and self-compassion. As you grew and experienced difficulties, your vessel became filled with stones—the stones of trials, mistakes, and pain.

These stones may feel like boulders that block the light, and you may sometimes feel frustrated. Though you may not always see the light within your vessel and you may miss that radiant light, it's there. Though the stones may have gotten in the way and you have spent countless hours trying to remove them without success, you are learning that there are better options. And, hopefully, those stones have helped you become resilient even when your mind says you aren't.

What Have the Stones Taught Me?

Take your time in answering the following questions.

- What do I want my life to stand for even when there are stones and boulders in my vessel of light?

- How are my values helping me with my struggles?

- What have I learned along this arduous journey?

- At this time, are my actions aligned with the person I want to become?

    - If so, what am I doing that shows this?

    - What strengths and talents am I using?

    - What values am I living as I face adversity?

> You are more than scrupulosity OCD
> and the struggles you experience.

Which Way Are you Going?

Paula's Story

Paula and her business partner had worked successfully together for eight years until, one day, her business partner began to question some of Paula's decisions. They began to disagree and eventually parted ways. Two years later, Paula discovered what seemed to have been her mistake and not her partner's, and she began to obsess about whether she had made other mistakes. She felt guilt and remorse, and she started ruminating on whether she might have done something illegal.

Because she was working hard at trying to figure things out, she believed she was living her values of integrity and justice. She didn't recognize that ruminating about whether she had broken the law was keeping her stuck in the scrupulosity trap. During treatment, she learned she had a choice. She could take action that got her closer to what mattered most in her life.

Keep Going on the Path Less Traveled

Every time you acknowledge and allow a difficult internal experience, are you doing it because there is a higher value (e.g., connection, creativity, love, independence, etc.)?

Your answers to the questions in the chart below can help you recognize if you are **moving away** (getting stuck in the scrupulosity trap) from your values or **moving toward** them.

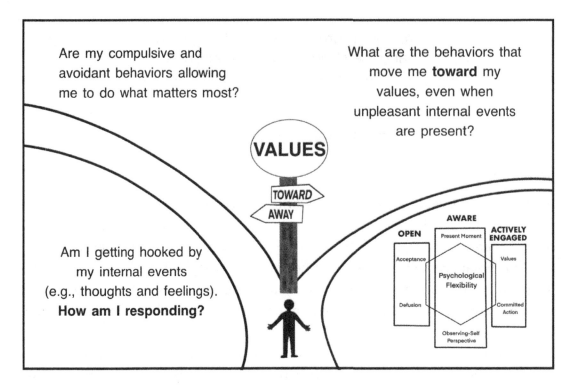

As you go about life, there will be days you won't be sure whether your actions are taking you toward or away from your values. As you continue to practice psychological flexibility (being open, aware, and actively engaged), you'll be able to recognize that you have a choice. You can take the path toward doing what matters most to you.

Take a photo of this graphic and carry it with you as a reminder.

How Do You Respond When You Get Hooked?

You may think you are behaving according to your values when you get hooked, but try to notice whether your behaviors are actually compulsions and then choose to move toward your values by living with flexibility amid the uncertainty.

Write down the skills you plan to use to live more flexibly each day.

Being Open

- How will I acknowledge and defuse from uncomfortable internal events?

- How will I apply the skills to allow the internal experiences, create space for them, and adopt a stance of willingness?

Being Aware

- How will I purposely advance to the present moment from day to day?

- How will I access my observing-self perspective and practice self-compassion skills?

Being Actively Engaged

- What are the values that make my heart sing and whole insides leap?

- How will I live these values daily?

13

Being Willing to Do What It Takes

Ben's Story

Ben's uncertainty about his fears coming true kept him stuck in the scrupulosity trap. When he insisted he could not bear the idea of accepting uncertainty for the rest of his life, his therapist shared the following metaphor.

The Two-Dial Radio

Life can be like a radio with two different dials—a discomfort dial and a willingness dial.[1]

No one likes pain or discomfort, but when you struggle with OCD, you may feel like you cannot tolerate going through life with uncertainty and other unpleasant internal events. You may say, "The discomfort is unbearable."

The Discomfort Dial

Wouldn't it be great if our bodies had a discomfort dial we could turn off when painful internal experiences show up? What if we could turn that dial to zero each time they do? Why don't we have one of those? Nature does not allow it. Dang.

The Willingness Dial

In reality, we have another dial. The willingness dial—a dial we can control. It's up to us to turn it on, especially when distressing internal events occur.

It would be ideal if we could be 100 percent willing to experience the difficult internal experiences that occur as we go about living a values-focused life. But it may not be realistic at this time. The good news is that we can use the willingness scale[2] (from zero to one hundred—resisting to befriending) to help us rate our willingness.

Notice the stages[3] of willingness as you continue to be open, aware, and actively engaged in what matters most in your life.

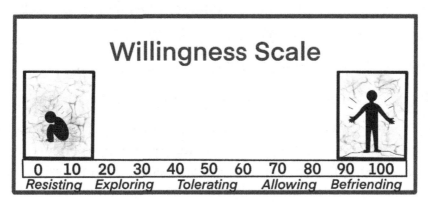

1. **Resisting:** The fighting that keeps you stuck in the scrupulosity trap. "I don't want to feel this way."

2. **Exploring:** Taking a curious approach and discovering what you may learn. "What would it be like to not push this feeling away?"

3. **Tolerating:** Trying and safely enduring. "I hate it, but I can endure a little longer."

4. **Allowing:** Practicing psychological-flexibility skills. "I'm noticing the sensation and can create space for it right now."

5. **Befriending:** Noticing the value of a difficult emotional experience. "What value may be on the other side of this struggle?"

You've Already Been Practicing Willingness

Have you noticed a willingness mindset in yourself in other areas of your life? Your scrupulous mind may not point that out. For example, you are willing to pay taxes even though you probably don't like doing it. If you are a parent, you are willing to get up in the middle of the night when your children are sick, even though you know you'll be exhausted the next day.

Why are you willing to do what it takes in these scenarios despite the discomfort? Because you have certain values. How about your willingness to allow unpleasant private events to run their natural course despite discomfort? Why is it worth it?

Here is a practice to help you in your quest for psychological flexibility so you can live your values from day to day.

Exercise 1. Willingness While You Read

- Choose a segment of text that usually gets you hooked or stuck.
- How willing are you to read something that triggers you? Decide how long you are willing to do it and how willing you are to experience any difficult feelings, thoughts, or other internal experiences that may arise. Indicate the percentage of willingness as shown on the scale above.
- While you read, your attention will likely drift. You may get hooked by something you've read. That's fine.
- Acknowledge this with a cognitive defusion skill ("Just got hooked. I'm not surprised." "There is a thought. Thank you, Mind.") and softly refocus on your reading.
- Notice your willingness and rate it throughout this practice.
- Choose an acceptance skill that will help you increase your willingness.
- When things get tough, remember what you value.
- Continue reading until you feel satisfied with your progress. You can also choose to keep going and see if you can increase your willingness.

How Did It Go?

- Were you able to finish your reading even if you got hooked?

- What psychological-flexibility skills did you implement?

- What were the values you remembered to help you keep going despite the difficulties?

- If you weren't triggered, is there something you can read that hooks you so you can practice the skills you've learned?

- Were you able to increase your willingness? If so, are you willing to repeat this activity and notice your willingness increase even more? If not, why not? Ponder your answers.

The next chapter will provide you with more opportunities to turn up your willingness dial and practice the psychological-flexibility skills you've been learning. Are you ready to take your willingness to a higher level?

14

Stepping into the River

Change is inevitable. Growth is optional.

—John C. Maxwell

I felt a tightness in my chest and a queasiness in my stomach when the river guide shared the rules and instructions for our adventure. I was anxious, no doubt. However, there was a higher value for me: adventure and curiosity.

When I do hard things (like writing this workbook!), I ask myself, "Why am I doing this hard thing? Why do I get myself into such challenging activities?" Then I remember, "Oh yeah. I value perseverance, service, caring, curiosity, and adventure."

Sometimes you may feel like you're stepping into a turbulent river and fear you will drown. Avoidance and compulsive behaviors could be the easy path, but even in turbulent waters, you can choose how you will go about living life.

ERP (exposure and response prevention) practice will allow you to recognize there is a higher value for what you are doing. You can respond to life's challenges with a flexible mindset and find peace.

Exposure and Response Prevention (ERP)

The gold standard treatment for obsessive-compulsive disorder is ERP. This means you learn to face the fears of the scrupulous mind and then choose to respond differently (response prevention). You knowingly choose to not give in to private or public compulsions (safety behaviors) that get you stuck in the OCD cycle.

As mentioned, ACT (acceptance and commitment therapy) is an exposure-based therapy. The psychological-flexibility skills you've learned throughout this workbook have given you the opportunity to observe and acknowledge your thoughts, feelings, and other internal experiences and respond in a more productive way. You've learned to view them with a different mindset, and hopefully this has helped you change your relationship with them. The coming values-based exposures will augment that learning.

As you engage in the exposures while applying the psychological-flexibility skills presented here, your relationship with your internal events will continue to change. However, this workbook does not replace treatment. **Please ask your treatment provider to assist you as you practice the willingness exercises (exposures) in this workbook.**

Exposure Practice Reminders

- When you willingly engage in exposures and apply psychological-flexibility skills, you will be able to disrupt the OCD cycle.

- Your mind will predict an increase in your fears. Yes, they may naturally escalate, especially when you get hooked and start fighting your thoughts and feelings. Remember, teaching your mind that you are in charge of your life is a process.

- As you apply psychological-flexibility skills, you will recognize that you have a choice as to how to respond.

- The more you focus on living with vitality and purpose, the less important the unpleasant and unwanted internal experiences will seem.

- The exposures you choose need to be connected to the obsessions ("If my friends knew how bad I am, they wouldn't want me around.") you struggle with already. You don't need to come up with "new obsessions" or do exposures unrelated to your lifestyle.

- Most importantly, the exposures need to match what you are yearning to do and haven't done (living your values) because of the OCD. You get to choose what exposures you'll do based on what you want your life to be about in the life domains you care about.

- Beware of the scrupulous mind providing a false sense of control. Its number-one job is to protect you. It will come to your rescue when you experience adversity and the uncertainty and anxiety feel unbearable. The sensible action might be to mentally reassure yourself by going back in time and ruminating. Instead, become open, aware, and actively engage in what matters most.

- Whatever you do to find relief from the internal experiences will most likely become a compulsion. Even your values ("I need be kind to everyone I meet."), skills, and exposures can turn into compulsions when you get hooked. Maintain a flexible outlook. Hold your values lightly. Watch out for rigidity in your everyday living.

- The scrupulous mind will do its best to find loopholes in your life. When you get stuck trying to figure out whether your actions are in the service of your values or OCD, you've likely gotten stuck in the OCD cycle. Create space for the uncertainty and gently get back to the present moment.

- When exposures become difficult and uncertainty becomes intolerable, acknowledge and allow the emotion and sensation related to the doubt and other internal events. Remember to treat yourself as you would a loved one and gently focus on what you are doing in the moment. Though the doubts won't go away, the unhelpful whispers of the scrupulous mind won't be as noisy or important.

- When doing exposures, it may "feel" like your clinician is disregarding your faith and other values. Clinicians who are appropriately trained to treat OCD will not ask you to challenge or disregard your values and principles. To avoid misunderstandings, provide appropriate release forms so your faith leader and treatment provider can communicate with one another. It's recommended that you, your treatment provider, and your faith leader have a joint session to ensure everyone is on the same page. Communication and collaboration are essential so you can receive the treatment you deserve.

  - When you "feel" like you are acting in opposition to your faith during exposures ("I can't allow these images. If I don't fight them, God will never forgive me."), that can be an indication of being hooked by the scrupulous mind. Consult with your treatment provider and continue to practice openness and awareness skills.

- Remember your religious beliefs and faith. Does the Creator know you have scrupulosity OCD? Would the Creator want you to receive help and do exposures so you can truly enjoy your faith?

You may be tossed from one thought to another, one emotion or sensation to another, **and** you can **still** act on what matters most.

Values-Based Exposures

As you live the life you want and become the person you want to become, unpleasant internal experiences (e.g., thoughts and feelings) will show up. Take the opportunity to find out for yourself that although those internal experiences may seem frightening, they are harmless. They don't have to be the focus of your life.

Engaging in life presents you with zillions of opportunities to either choose to listen to the scrupulous mind or move toward what matters most despite discomfort. This chapter is an invitation to apply psychological-flexibility skills when your mind utters scary thoughts.

You have been practicing skills to be **open** to your internal experiences, create space for them when they are present, and acknowledge them for what they are: natural internal events that come and go.

The **awareness** skills you've been implementing will strengthen your ability to connect to the here and now instead of getting stuck in the scrupulosity trap. When life's storms roll in, you can remember that you are not alone. Every human being experiences pain and suffering. Your loved ones and God can be with you every step of the way. Treat yourself as you would a struggling loved one.

You can be *imperfectly good* and find joy as you become **actively engaged** in living your values and doing what causes your whole insides to leap.

Remember, when you live your values, you are choosing to move your feet, hands, and mouth to do and say what matters. Your values are not guided by the scrupulous mind or what others say you should be doing or saying in your life. Acting on your values will allow you to be open to new things, willing to experience discomfort, and focused on the present moment (see chapter 2).

Go ahead and write down your top five values and get ready to apply psychological-flexibility skills as you purposely practice exposures. As you go about your day and distress shows up, you can remember why the discomfort is worth (your values) having in that moment.

My Top 5 Values
1.
2.
3.
4.
5.

List the life domains most relevant to your life (refer to the chart you completed at the end of chapter 7) and add them here along with the values (top five or more values) you wish to live in those domains. For example:

Life Domains	Values
Relationships	*Being loving/Connecting*
Education/Work	*Being responsible and dependable*
Personal Growth/Health	*Learning/Being fit*
Spirituality	*Connecting with Deity/Serving*
Recreation/Leisure	*Adventure*

These lists will come in handy as you plan your exposures practices.

Life Domains	Values

Jon's Story

During treatment, Jon said, "I'm able to get unhooked from my thoughts. I get it. They are just thoughts. But my sensations are real, and I cannot live the rest of my life feeling like I'm drowning in dry land. How on earth can I embrace that sensation when I can't even tolerate it?"

Can you identify with Jon? No one likes to experience unpleasant sensations, and the urge to fight them is understandable, but doing so is not the answer to living a joy-filled life. We interpret sensations as necessary or unpleasant according to the situations in which we find ourselves.

For example, when you engage in any kind of exercise, you may experience heart palpitations, shortness of breath, sweaty limbs, muscle tension, and fatigue, and yet you're not alarmed by these physical sensations.

On the other hand, when your scrupulous mind insists your thoughts could become reality or you won't be able to live with uncertainty, sensations similar to those mentioned above may arise, but they feel threatening instead of natural. And so you begin to resist them.

Facing Unpleasant Bodily Sensations (Interoceptive Exposures)

As you practice these exposures, you will be intentionally bringing on the physical symptoms your mind links to anxiety, uncertainty, shame, guilt, and other internal experiences. And you will learn how to respond differently (e.g., make room for these sensations and symptoms while they are present) instead of giving in to private or public compulsions

The goal of these exposures is for your mind and body to learn that even though the unpleasant sensations or symptoms are present, you are not in imminent danger. You can let them be there and focus on what matters in the present moment. You can recognize that they come and go and that you don't have to submit, ignore, or fight them.

The unpleasant bodily sensations may appear to be dangerous (e.g., abdominal pain or sudden heart palpitations) because your language machine is trying to protect you. You will learn how to disrupt the expectancy your mind and body have around these sensations.

The practices will help you change your relationship with uncomfortable and unwanted bodily sensations. Are you ready and willing?

If you're just curious, that's a great start. Give them a try. If you find it difficult at first, take a break and come back to them later. The duration and frequency of these practices can make a difference. Learning to increase your willingness and changing your relationship with the distressing sensations is possible; you've been training for this!

Exercise 1. Allowing Unpleasant Bodily Sensations

Plan to go through all the exercises listed on the chart[1] below at your earliest convenience so that you can choose exercises that target the sensations you find intolerable or unpleasant.

You'll need several small cocktail-sized straws, a swivel chair, stairs, water, and, most importantly, curiosity and willingness.

There may be other exercises that evoke unpleasant sensations that are not listed. Use your creativity to intentionally generate those sensations and add them to your interoceptive-exposures practices.

For example, if you experience a heaviness in your chest, you could lie down and place heavy blankets, books, or other objects on your chest to simulate that unwanted sensation.

Go ahead and follow the instructions below. There will be additional instructions later on. See what you can learn now.

Exercise	Description and Duration	Your Experience
Breathe through a small, cocktail-sized straw.	Using the straw, pinch your nose and breathe through it as long as possible; take a quick breath and repeat for at least 60 seconds. Do a minimum of two trials.	
Swallow quickly.	Without drinking water, swallow as quickly as possible ten consecutive times.	

Exercise	Description and Duration	Your Experience
Shake your head from side to side.	Rotate your head from shoulder to shoulder at a rate of two or more rotations per second for 30 seconds.	
Place your head between your legs.	Place your head between your legs while sitting in a chair for 30 seconds.	
Run in place or run/walk up and down a flight of stairs.	Jog at rapid pace, keeping your knees high for 60 seconds, or run/walk up and down the stairs twenty times.	
Hyperventilate.	Take rapid, deep breaths without stopping at a rate of one breath every two seconds; do this for 60 seconds.	
Hold your breath.	Pinch your nose and hold your breath as long as possible; take a quick breath and repeat. Do this for at least 60 seconds and a minimum of two trials.	
Spin around and around.	While sitting or standing, spin at rate of one rotation every two seconds; do this for 60 seconds.	
Do push-ups	Either hold a push-up position (plank) or repeat push-ups, depending on your level of strength; do this for 60 seconds.	

Now you know which exercises simulate the particular sensation you find intolerable and distressing. For example, as Jon went through each of them, the straw-breathing exercise reminded him of the sensations related to his intrusive thoughts, and he realized he could practice this exposure to change his relationship with those sensations and thoughts.

As you participate in these exercises, be attentive to what's happening and do your best to not give in to public or private compulsive and/or avoidant behaviors.

> When you intentionally create a situation that naturally brings up unpleasant sensations, you can disrupt the expectancy your mind has around them.

Set aside a few minutes every day to practice the exercises that target the feared sensations. Then, if you wish to enhance your learning, start adding another activity that might also evoke that particular sensation. For example, Jon practiced the straw-breathing exercise while reading an article on his smartphone that brought up his feared intrusive thoughts and unwanted sensations. He responded with psychological-flexibility skills.

Notice the actions you choose to take before, during, and after the exposures. Are you being flexible or rigid? These practices will allow you to respond differently to scrupulosity and other life storms.

Write down your plan to practice psychological-flexibility skills, then note what you learned after engaging in the activity.

1. **Mind's Predictions**
    - Before engaging in the interoceptive exposure, write down what your mind predicts will happen before, during, and after the exposure (e.g., "If I breathe through a small straw while pinching my nose, I may pass out and ruin my whole day!").

2. **Write Your Fear Down**
    - What do you fear will happen as you experience these bodily sensations and other unpleasant thoughts? What is your mind saying? ("My fears will come true because I'm feeling this way.")

Indicate how you'll respond before and during the exposures.

3. **Be Open**
    - Adopt a willingness stance. Notice where you are on the willingness scale before, during, and after the practice.

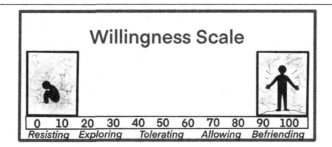

- **Resisting:** The fighting that keeps you stuck in the scrupulosity trap.
- **Exploring:** Taking a curious approach and discovering what you may learn.
- **Tolerating:** Trying and safely enduring.
- **Allowing:** Practicing openness and awareness skills.
- **Befriending:** Noticing the value of a difficult emotional experience.

- Acknowledge your sensations and other internal experiences (e.g., "I am noticing shortness of breath.").
- Allow your sensations and other experiences to be present ("I can make room for this sensation.").

4. **Be Aware**
   - Advance to the present moment and remember your values (e.g., living independently). Are these practices worth doing because you care about living with vitality?

5. **Be Actively Engaged**
   - Stay focused on the exposure and remember what matters most—your values. Why is this practice worth doing?

6. **Note What You Learned by Doing This Activity**
   - Was it as your mind predicted? What was your mind saying during the practice? What did you learn from it? Are you ready to apply willingness in your everyday living?

Jon's Activity Chart

1. **Mind's Prediction**	*I might be able to breathe through a straw for 20 seconds. It's going to be tough!*
2. **What Is My Fear?**	*If I don't fight the sensations and other internal experiences, I might act on my intrusive thoughts.*

How Will I Respond?

3. **Be Open**	
• Adopt a willingness stance. Where is my willingness?	*I'm curious and probably at a 9 on the willingness scale.*
• Acknowledge my sensations and other internal experiences	*I'll acknowledge what's happening by saying, "This is tough."*
• Allow my sensations and other internal experiences	*Not sure if I'm ready to make room for those ugly sensations, even though I sort of practiced some of these exercises in chapter 7.*
4. **Be Aware**	
• Advance to the present moment	*I'll try to stay focused on the activity.*
5. **Be Actively Engaged**	*As I focus on the activity, I'll be willing to experience discomfort and make room for it because I want to start attending my religious services.*
6. **Note What I Learned**	*I'm surprised I was able to do this practice twice in a row. I realized this is not as hard as my mind told me it would be. I am willing to try this exercise again. Then I'll be ready to combine it while playing with my kids.*

Interoceptive Exposures Activity Chart

1. **Mind's Prediction**	
2. **What Is My Fear?**	

How Will I Respond?

3. **Be Open**	
• Adopt a willingness stance. Where is my willingness?	
• Acknowledge the sensations and other internal experiences	
• Allow my sensations and other internal experiences	
4. **Be Aware**	
• Advance to the present moment	
5. **Be Actively Engaged**	
6. **Note What I Learned**	

Go to mindsetfamilytherapy.com to download all the exercise charts for this chapter.

Repeat the practices as often as you'd like. Are you able to increase your willingness as you repeat them? Is there anything you'd like to change (e.g., location, frequency, or intensity of the practices) to increase your learning? Later in this chapter, you'll be able to combine interoceptive exposures with other types of exposures.

Take a photo of the following summary so you have it handy on your smartphone, and practice whenever life presents you with opportunities to respond with flexibility.

> Allowing Unpleasant Bodily Sensations
> 1. Notice My Mind's Predictions
> 2. Notice My Fears
> 3. Be Open
>   - Adopt a willingness stance
>   - Acknowledge my sensations and other internal events
>   - Allow my sensations and other internal events
> 4. Be Aware
>   - Advance to the present moment
> 5. Be Actively Engaged
>   - Stay focused on the exposure and remember my values
> 6. What Did I Learn?

No matter what activities you engage in, your mind will continue to provide helpful and unhelpful advice, **and** you get to choose how to respond (chart below) to your internal experiences. As you make decisions, keep your values front and center. They'll help you choose the road less traveled.

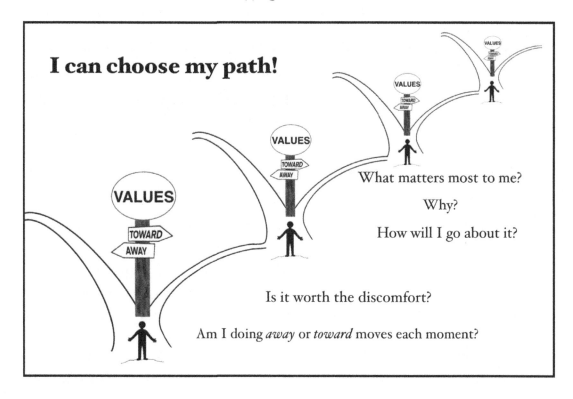

Take a photo of this chart so it's available when you need it. **Remember, your choices are ongoing.**

Imaginal Exposures

Allie's Story

Allie's constant battle with her blasphemous thoughts related to Deity and spiritual leaders left her feeling exhausted. "How can I know God will forgive me? I can't do this."

But step by step, she learned how to be flexible and change her relationship with uncertainty by writing scripts of uncertainty and doing imaginal exposures.

Situations in which imaginal exposures are most helpful:

- When an in-vivo (real-time) exposure is not practical because the feared consequence is in the distant future. ("I won't make it to heaven.")

- When your obsessions and uncertainty about a distant past experience have hijacked your life. ("I can't sleep just thinking I might have cheated on my taxes ten years ago. I need to call the IRS.")

- When in-vivo exposures are too difficult and not feasible at a given time. ("I may lose my mind and purposely crash the car while my kids are in the back seat.")

- When you want to strengthen your flexibility skills before you do in-vivo exposures.

Struggling with unwanted thoughts, ideas, images, memories, and doubts that don't match the person you are and want to become can be overwhelming. ("Why can't I stop those inappropriate images? Does it mean I want them?")

When you have an internal experience that repeats itself, you may believe that if you don't give in to the compulsive behavior, your fear may come true. When you choose to revisit (purposeful exposure) such an internal experience and practice psychological-flexibility skills, you'll find you don't have to be ruled by the scrupulous mind. You'll discover you can choose to live your values despite the unpleasant internal experiences.

Exercise 2. Values-Based Scripts of Uncertainty

As mentioned, there are times when you will need to practice imaginal exposures. Writing a script will enhance your learning and the opportunity to apply the psychological-flexibility skills you've been practicing.

In the chart below, list the most prominent obsessions you experience on a daily basis. This list will remind you to write scripts and practice the imaginal exposures in this section.

For example:

Obsessions

Why can't I stop seeing these awful images?
I feel joy when I serve. Am I being selfish?
Did I mean to offend my friend?
I may have cheated on my taxes.
Am I going to hurt my kids?
Am I sinning? Will God punish me?

Obsessions

Before preparing your script, let's review pertinent information regarding mental compulsions.

Mental (Private) Compulsions

- Remember, **anything you do to find relief** from uncertainty and other internal events, including ruminating about a past or future event, trying to figure things out, and mentally reassuring yourself, **is a compulsion.**

- When you struggle with private compulsions in response to the obsessions related to scrupulosity or other themes of OCD, you'll find it's considerably difficult to not give in to those compulsions.

- You know what happens when you try to ignore and fight a thought or other internal experience. In order to *not* think about it, you *have* to think about it (see chapter 3). The good news is that as you engage in doing exposures, you can increase your awareness around what your mind is saying and recognize you have a choice in how you respond.

- A mental compulsion can happen in less than a millisecond. "If it's that fast, then how can I prevent the compulsion?" clients often ask in frustration. That's a legitimate question, and the good news is that there are actions you can choose to decrease and eventually eliminate these compulsions.

- Make a conscious effort to practice awareness skills. As you practice connecting to the present moment (see chapter 9), you will be able to recognize the obsessions and respond with openness and willingness instead of reacting with a private compulsion. Be patient and flexible with your practices. Focus on the process instead of expecting immediate results.

- Whenever you recognize you're stuck in the scrupulosity trap, take a moment to acknowledge what has happened ("I just got hooked by trying to figure out if I really sinned ten years ago."). Then create space for the feeling that is present in the moment ("I can make space for uncertainty.") and gently reshift your focus to what you were doing that mattered in that moment. As the mind insists on its unhelpful advice, continue to practice your skills and advance to the present moment.

- As you purposely think of the core fear during imaginal exposures, you have the opportunity to use phrases of uncertainty and listen to your script while allowing the unpleasant emotion, sensation, or other internal experience instead of giving in to the compulsions.

- When it comes to doubt, obsessing and ruminating will not solve the uncertainty. What counts is what you do with your feet and hands and what you say. Notice your toward and away moves (see end of chapters 2 and 12).

Preparing Your Script

To write your script, include the following information in the preparation chart:

- **Obsessions** ("Am I sinning?" "Will God punish me?")

- **Compulsions** you won't give in to while doing exposures (e.g., ruminating, confessing, praying)

- **Core feared consequence.** What is your greatest fear should you not be able to engage in the compulsions? Allie didn't like experiencing anxiety, uncertainty, and shame. However, once she asked herself additional questions (as outlined below), she discovered her ultimate/core fear was not making it to heaven.

    To find out what your **core fear** is, ask yourself these types of questions:
    "If I am not able to (name the compulsion), I fear (what may happen), and if this is true, then what? Keep asking this question ("And if this is true,

then what?") until you can't think of anything else you fear. If the fear last mentioned is causing you the highest distress and you can't come up with additional fears, you've found your core feared consequence.

- **The value/s related to the situation** you want to live (e.g., connecting to God) despite the discomfort.
- **Acknowledge how you feel as you write your script.** ("I don't think I can live with this uncertainty anymore.")
- **State how you'll allow unwanted feelings and other difficult internal experiences** as you do the exposure. ("I can hold shame as if it were a wounded creature.")

Allie's Script Preparation Chart

Obsessions	*Why can't I stop these blasphemous thoughts? Am I sinning? Will God forgive me?*
Compulsions	*I'll refrain from praying, confessing, and figuring out my thoughts.*
Core feared consequence	*If I don't give in to my compulsions, I fear I'll feel anxious and uncertain I'm doing the right thing* (obvious feared consequences). *If this is true, then what? Then I don't care about God. And if this is true, then what? I am a bad person. And if this is true, then what? God will punish me. If this is true, then what?* **I won't make it to heaven.**
Value/s related to the situation	*Connecting with God.*
Acknowledge the thoughts and other internal experiences on your script.	*I'm not sure I can prevent my compulsions. I can't tolerate the uncertainty.*
Willingness to allow uncertainty and other internal experiences during the exposure	*I'll recognize that I can't be perfectly good and create space for uncertainty at the same time.*
Review script	✔
Record script	✔

Allie's Script

I'm constantly sinning because I cannot control my blasphemous thoughts (obsession). *If I choose to no longer pray, confess, and figure out my thoughts* (compulsions), *God will be angry at me and not let me into heaven* (core fear). *This uncertainty seems unbearable* (acknowledging internal experiences), *but I want to connect with God* (value), *so I will work on creating space for uncertainty, recognize that I am imperfectly good, and let Him be my judge* (willingness).

Allie chose to write a script targeting her core fear, state her willingness, and allow the uncertainty to be present because she cared about connecting with God. Her willingness to listen to her scripts and practice imaginal exposures helped her discover that she could disrupt the scrupulous mind's expectancy when it told her, "You can't survive or even tolerate this doubt!"

The elements of your script don't need to be in the order listed. You can write your script on your smartphone or get a small notebook to keep all your scripts together. You can also go to mindsetfamilytherapy.com to download the exposure forms and charts.

Values-Based Script Preparation Chart

Obsessions	
Compulsions	
Core feared consequence	

Value/s related to the situation	
Acknowledge your thoughts and other internal experiences	
Willingness to allow uncertainty and other internal experiences during the exposure	
Review script	
Record script	

Once you have written your script, read through it several times and make the necessary changes so that the words create the feelings and sensations you'd experience when triggered by external or internal experiences.

Then record the script on your smartphone's recording app. Repeat it several times so it lasts five to ten minutes.

Write Your Script

Now you are ready for imaginal exposures. When you engage in imaginal exposures, you can literally imagine your core feared consequence is happening right then. Focusing on that fear will most likely hook you. That's okay. As soon as you notice you've been hooked, go ahead and practice your favorite psychological-flexibility skills (see chapter 12), including making room for uncertainty and other emotions and sensations that might arise in that moment.

Though it may feel like you can't tolerate or allow the unpleasant internal experiences, refrain from giving in to compulsive or avoidant behaviors and respond with psychological-flexibility skills instead.

Exercise 3. Imaginal-Exposure Practice

Set aside enough time to do this practice the first time. You can lengthen the time as you continue to move up the willingness scale and practice two to three times daily.

1. **Listen to the script you've prepared** (per instructions above).

2. **Write down what your mind is predicting will happen during and after the exposure.** ("I may have a panic attack during the exposure." "I'll be obsessing all day.")

3. **As you listen to the script, imagine your core feared consequence.**
   - For example, every time Allie listened to her script, she imagined facing God and being denied entrance into heaven. This, of course, was her usual obsession; however, this time she was doing it with a confident mindset.

Indicate how you'll respond before and during the exposures.

4. **Be open.**
   - Adopt a willingness stance so you can lean into the discomfort instead of looking to lower your anxiety and uncertainty. Mark where your willingness is before the exposure (e.g., 20 percent). Also note how long you are willing to do the exposure (e.g., fifteen seconds, ten minutes, or thirty minutes).

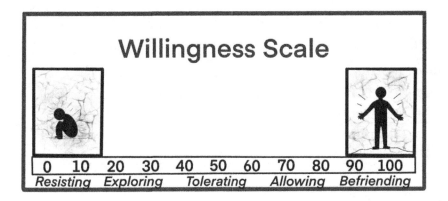

- Acknowledge your internal experiences. ("I am noticing uncertainty.")
- Allow the internal experiences. ("I can make room for anxiety.")

5. **Be aware.**
    - Advance to the present moment after acknowledging and allowing your internal events. Gently refocus on the task at hand (e.g., the exposure).
    - Access your observing-self perspective and remember to treat yourself as you would a loved one who is struggling. Use the self-compassion mantra you prepared in chapter 11.

6. **Be actively engaged in what matters most.**
    - Remember your values during the exposures. Is this exposure worth doing because you care about living a meaningful life (e.g., connecting with friends)? Act on your values every day despite the discomfort you may face each moment.

7. **Note what you learned.**
    - Write what you learned about yourself and your internal events after the activity. Was it as your mind predicted? Were you able to turn your willingness dial on? If so, for how long? How high were you able to move on the willingness scale? Were you able to be open, aware, and actively engaged in the activity? Did your relationship with uncertainty and other internal experiences change? If so, how? If not, what else can you do? **After the exposures, note how you will go about (e.g., being flexible and acting on your values) the rest of the day.**

Allie's Imaginal Exposure Chart

Allie used this chart to help her remember her psychological-flexibility skills.

1. **Listen to My Script**	✔
2. **Mind's Prediction During and After the Exposure**	*I won't be able to tolerate listening to the script. I may have a panic attack.*
3. **Core Fear I'll Imagine during the Exposure**	*Facing God and being denied heaven.*

How Will I Respond?

4. **Be Open**	
• Adopt a willingness stance	*Right now, my willingness is a twenty. I don't think it can go higher. I can only do this for ten minutes.*
• Acknowledge my internal experiences	*I'll use phrases of uncertainty: "You may be right, Mind. This stinks. Yup!"*
• Allow my internal experiences	*I'll create space for uncertainty.*
5. **Be Aware**	
• Advance to the present moment	*When my mind distracts me or hooks me, I will acknowledge and allow the internal events to be there and gently shift my attention back to the present moment (listening to the script and imagining my core fear).*
• Access my observing-self perspective and remember my self-compassion mantra	*I'll say my mantra, "Allowing uncertainty is painful. I know God is aware of my suffering. Others experience similar emotions. God is kind. I can be kind with myself too."*
6. **Be Actively Engaged in What Matters Most**	*This exposure is worth doing because I want to connect with God in different ways even when feeling anxious and uncertain.*
7. **Note What I Learned**	*My willingness went up to 40 percent. Maintained my willingness for ten minutes, though at times I wanted to quit. I didn't have a panic attack but felt anxious the whole time. I'm still feeling a lot of uncertainty, but it seems I can tolerate it. I will continue to practice my flexibility skills while I visit with friends tonight.*

Imaginal Exposure Chart

Right before starting your imaginal exposure, jot down your plan. You'll find that this step will enhance your learning and willingness. As you engage in the exposure, remember to be open, aware, and actively engaged in this activity. When you are done with the exposure, complete step 7.

1. **Listen to My Script**	
2. **Mind's Predictions**	
3. **Core Fear I'll Imagine during the Exposure**	

How Will I Respond?

4. **Be Open**	
• Adopt a willingness stance. Where is my willingness before the exposure? How long can I do the exposure?	
• Acknowledge my internal experiences	
• Allow my internal experiences	

5. **Be Aware**	
• Advance to the present moment	
• Access my observing-self perspective and remember my self-compassion mantra	
6. **Be Actively Engaged in What Matters Most**	
7. **Note What I Learned**	

During exposures and in everyday life, be attentive to what psychological-flexibility skills you can utilize in response to what's happening in that moment. For example, you may be allowing an unpleasant sensation and notice you've gotten hooked. Take a few moments to acknowledge (e.g., "I'm noticing I'm having a judgmental thought. Thanks Mind!") it. Then advance to the present moment. The mind may persist in getting you hooked with a thought, feeling, or other internal experience. Gently acknowledge and defuse. You may choose to silently recite your self-compassion mantra and advance back to the present moment. Use the skills at any given time and try to maintain a flexible attitude.

> Beware of turning exposures into compulsions.
> When doing any kind of exposure, have a *"Bring it on!"* mindset, not a ruminating mentality. The difference between rumination and willingly imagining your feared consequence is being open, aware, and actively engaged in what matters most to you.

Take a picture of the willingness scale and the imaginal-exposure steps to have them handy on your smartphone.

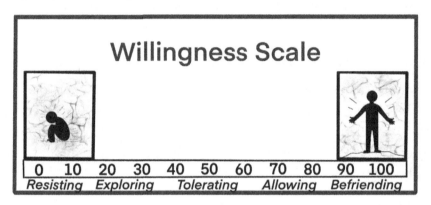

Imaginal Exposures in Brief

1. Prepare and Listen to My Script
2. Write Mind's Prediction
3. Imagine Core Feared Consequence
4. Be Open
   - Adopt a willingness stance
   - Acknowledge my internal experiences
   - Allow my internal experiences and create space for them
5. Be Aware
   - Advance to the present moment
   - Access my observing-self perspective and remember my self-compassion mantra
6. Be Actively Engaged in What Matters Most. Why Is the Exposure Worth Doing?
7. Note What I Learned

"Bring It On!" Activities
(Real-Time or In-Vivo Exposures)

Miles' Story

Miles was constantly worried about consuming animal products and contributing to animal cruelty. He genuinely believed his daily compulsions were his only option when it came to living his values (e.g., being kind to people and animals). He didn't realize that his compulsive behaviors were actually moving him away from what mattered most to him.

When he was ready and willing to do the in-vivo, values-based exposures, he improved his psychological-flexibility skills.

Exercise 4. In-Vivo Exposures

You've been practicing how to be open, aware, and actively engaged in life. You've been developing a different relationship with your internal experiences. In-vivo exposures will enhance that learning and continue to create new neural pathways (see chapter 1). You'll recognize that you no longer need to avoid living the life you care about!

Additional Reminders

- When you get frustrated and/or hooked with unpleasant internal events, remember what you can truly control in your life –your response to what is happening. You can choose what to do with your hands and feet, and what you say.

- In your everyday life, when you get distracted by unhelpful internal experiences, remember that you do have a choice on where to focus. You can decide to be here with what matters or there (stuck in the scrupulosity trap).

- Leaning in and sitting with the uncertainty means being willing to breathe it in and making space for it in your body. Please see chapters 7–12 to review other ways you can allow uncertainty and other internal experiences when they are present.

- Be intentional about doing exposures and remind yourself why the discomfort is worth having.

Preparation Chart

List an activity you desire to engage in because of what you value. Write down the compulsive and avoidant behaviors you won't give in to as you live your values in the areas of life (relationships, education/work, personal growth/health, spirituality, recreation/leisure) you wish to thrive in as shown below.

Action I Will Take	Compulsive and Avoidant Behaviors I Won't Give in to	Life Domain	Values I Want to Live
Go to the gym	Won't over clean equipment or avoid people	Personal Growth/Health	Being fit
Attend religious services	Repenting prayers Ruminating	Spirituality	Connecting with Deity

Write down your plan to practice psychological-flexibility skills. Then note what you learned after engaging in the activity.

1. **Mind's predictions.**

   - Before engaging in the activity you've chosen, write down what your mind predicts will happen during and after the exposure. ("My mind is saying I won't be able to tolerate the anxiety." "I may just give up.")

2. **Indicate your core feared consequence.**

   - ("I'll become a despicable human being who doesn't care about living creatures.") It's helpful to know your core feared consequence when doing in-vivo exposures.

Indicate how you'll respond to your internal experiences before, during, and after the exposures.

3. **Be open.**

   - Adopt a willingness stance as you live your value in the area you've chosen. Lean into the discomfort. Mark where your willingness is before the exposure (e.g., 10 percent). Also note how long are you willing to do the exposure (e.g., fifteen minutes).

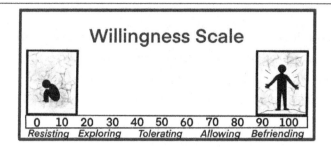

- **Resisting:** The fighting that keeps you stuck in the scrupulosity trap.
- **Exploring:** Taking a curious approach and discovering what you may learn.
- **Tolerating:** Trying and safely enduring.
- **Allowing:** Practicing openness and awareness skills.
- **Befriending:** Noticing the value of a difficult emotional experience.

- Acknowledge your internal events during the activity. You can listen to the whole script you prepared or just part of it. ("I am noticing the thought that I may become a despicable human being.") You can also use phrases of uncertainty depending on the activity. ("Mind, you could be right. We'll have to see.")

- Allow the internal experiences to be present by practicing willingness skills. ("I can create space for shame in my body.")

4. **Be aware.**

   - Advance to the present moment after acknowledging and allowing your internal events. Gently refocus on the task at hand—in this case, the activity you're engaged in because of what you value.

   - Access your observing-self perspective and remember to treat yourself as you would a loved one who is struggling. Use the self-compassion mantra you prepared in chapter 11. ("I am noticing shame. Others struggle with similar emotions. I'm not alone. I can be patient with myself right now.")

5. **Be actively engaged in what matters most.**
   - Act on your values despite the discomfort in the moment. ("This activity / exposure is worth doing because I care about connecting with friends.")

6. **Note what you learned.**
   - After the activity, write what you learned about yourself and your internal experiences. Was it as your mind predicted? Were you able to turn your willingness dial on and for how long? If you were able to turn it on, how high were you able to move on the willingness scale? Were you able to be open, aware, and actively engaged in the activity? Did your relationship with uncertainty and other internal events change? If so, how? If not, what else can you do?

Miles' Preparation Chart

Miles chose to refrain from reading labels, ruminating, and avoiding people whenever he went to the grocery store. He wanted to connect with people because he cared about being kind.

Action I Will Take	Compulsive and Avoidant Behaviors I Won't Give in to	Life Domain	Values I Want to Live
Grocery shopping	Reading labels Ruminating Avoiding people	Relationships	Being kind

Miles' Activity Chart

1. **Mind's Predictions**	*I won't be able to handle the anxiety and shame. I may end up giving in to my compulsions as usual.*
2. **Core Fear I'll Imagine During the Exposure**	*I may become a despicable human being who doesn't care about living creatures.*

How Will I Respond?

3. **Be Open**	
• Adopt a willingness stance	*Right now, my willingness is a 10. It may go to 20 percent. I don't know. I'll go shopping and finish no matter how long it takes me.*
• Acknowledge internal experiences	*I'll agree with my core fear: "I will become a despicable human being who doesn't care about people or animals. I'll just have to see." I will also say yes to the mind no matter what it says as I shop.*
• Allow internal experiences	*Breathe in shame and allow it to stay without giving in to my regular compulsions, even though I don't like it.*
4. **Be Aware**	
• Advance to the present moment	*I'll smile and say hi to at least five people instead of getting stuck in my rituals.*
• Access my observing-self perspective and remember my self-compassion mantra	*Mantra: "I'm noticing shame. Others struggle with similar emotions. I'm not alone. I can be patient with myself right now."*
5. **Be Actively Engaged in What Matters Most**	*As I shop, I'll be friendly and kind to those I meet because I care.*
6. **Note What I Learned**	*My willingness went up to 20 percent; I was anxious the whole time and managed to smile and greet a couple of people. I came home feeling anxious but with a sense of accomplishment because I didn't behave compulsively. I think I can do this and continue to be flexible the rest of the day.*

Preparation Chart

List an activity and the compulsive and avoidant behaviors you won't give in to as you live your values in the domains of life (relationships, education/work, personal growth/health, spirituality, recreation/leisure) you wish to enjoy.

Stepping into the River

Action I Will Take	Compulsive and Avoidant Behaviors I Won't Give in to	Life Domain	Values I Want to Live

Action I Will Take	Compulsive and Avoidant Behaviors I Won't Give in to	Life Domain	Values I Want to Live

Activity Chart

Write down your plan to practice psychological-flexibility skills before, during and after the exposure. Then note what you learned.

1. **Mind's Predictions**	
2. **Core Fear I'll Imagine During the Exposure**	

How Will I Respond?

3. **Be Open**	
• Adopt a willingness stance	
• Acknowledge internal experiences	
• Allow internal experiences	
4. **Be Aware**	
• Advance to the present moment	

• Access my observing-self perspective and remember my self-compassion mantra	
5. **Be Actively Engaged in What Matters Most**	
6. **Note What I Learned**	

Go to mindsetfamilytherapy.com to download all the charts in this chapter.

Consider repeating your values-based exposures as often as you can to promote changes in your relationship with your internal experiences (e.g., uncertainty). You can move toward your values every day by honing your psychological-flexibility skills!

Mixing Things Up

All growth starts at the end of your comfort zone.

—*Tony Robbins*[2]

Miles' Story Continued

Miles was invited to combine the different types of exposures[3] (i.e., bodily sensations, imaginal, and in-vivo) as well as change time, location, event, and people to strengthen his learning and ability to change his relationship with external (e.g., hearing the news about animal cruelty) and internal experiences (e.g., anxiety and uncertainty).

When he went to the grocery store **(real-time exposures)**, he would remember his core feared consequence and act on what was most important to him by greeting people instead of giving in to his rituals. He would also practice openness and awareness skills as needed. When he got home, he would run up and down four flights of stairs **(bodily-sensation exposures)**, then sit and imagine himself ten years older and being heartless and mean toward the animals and people around him **(imaginal exposure)**.

He didn't like doing the exposures, but he cared more about living his values. Like Miles, you can decide what areas of your life you've neglected and plan activities that can help you get back to living the life you want to live.

> Purposeful exposure practice is
> learning how to respond flexibly to life's pain-filled gifts.

Combining Values-Based Exposures

You can combine these bodily-sensation, imaginal, and in-vivo exposures consecutively as well as change the order, location, time, event, and people. The more you mix things up, the more flexible you can become as you encounter triggers throughout the day.

Miles' Mix-It Up Chart

Life Domain	Values	Bodily-Sensation Exposure	Imaginal Exposure	In-Vivo Exposure
Relationships	Caring and kindness	Run up and down four flights of stairs	Script: I may become a despicable human being.	Go to grocery store and interact with people

Look at the examples in the chart below, then decide what life domains and values you wish to address because they are important to you. You may also list the compulsions you wish to abstain from in a particular area of your life that's important to you, then randomly pick one activity and go for it.

Proceed according to the instructions shared for each type of exposure and decide how you will mix things up to improve your learning.

Example of a Mix-It-Up Chart

Life Domain	Values	Bodily-Sensation Exposure	Imaginal Exposure	In-Vivo Exposure
Relationships	Love		Script: loyalty to spouse when I watch movies	Watch movie with spouse and accept the uncertainty that I may not be a faithful partner when I admire someone's beauty
Education/ Work	Confidence	Spin on swivel chair	Script: uncertainty I may be cheating	
Personal Growth/Health	Fitness	Run up and down the stairs	Script: risk of having sexual thoughts	Go to gym and risk noticing immodestly dressed people
Spirituality	Connection with God	Twenty jumping jacks		Read scriptures despite anxiety and fear of offending God
Recreation/ Leisure	Fun	Shake head from side to side		Go to party with friends and risk offending someone

Mix-It-Up Chart

Life Domain	Values	Bodily-Sensation Exposure	Imaginal Exposure	In-Vivo Exposure

As you go about your day, make a conscious effort to delay, change, or replace your compulsions by applying the psychological-flexibility skills you've learned.

Visit this site for a video (*The OCD Mind and Uncertainty/ACT*) I produced to help clients remember that it is possible to live a joyful life despite OCD: https://www.youtube.com/watch?v=hIUkN59EtQo.

The psychological-flexibility skills you've learned in this workbook will help you get unstuck from the scrupulosity-OCD trap and any themes OCD may target. **You can also use these skills every day with life's other challenges.** You now have the tools to respond differently and keep moving toward what matters most to you, and be willing to be imperfectly good!

You are taking the path less traveled. Remember, creating new brain pathways takes time and effort. Be patient. Live with vitality and peace instead of worry and uncertainty.

Take a photo of the chart below. Keep it handy on your smartphone and continue moving toward your values!

Engage in Life Every Day!

I Can Be:
1. **Open**
   - Adopt a willingness stance
   - Acknowledge my internal experiences
   - Allow my internal experiences
2. **Aware**
   - Advance to the present moment
   - Access my observing self-mode and practice self-compassion
3. **Actively engaged in what matters most**

What am I learning when I practice psychological-flexibility skills?

Invitation

What changes can you make to improve your values-based exposures? Remember your values are the beacon among life's turbulent waters.

15

Going Beyond What You See

"You have forgotten who you are. Look inside yourself, Simba."[1] These powerful lines spoken by Mufasa in the Disney classic *The Lion King* apply here because scrupulosity OCD can cause you to forget who you are. Simba ran away from his troubles. Because his guilt and shame were too painful, he chose to escape. He found some friends who taught him how to live an "easy" life—no troubles, no problems. But, as we now know, avoidance is never a long-term solution.

Rafiki the baboon helped Simba reconnect with his values and what his father had taught him: "Remember who you are . . . remember . . . remember."

You don't need to have a royal heritage, like Simba, to become the best version of yourself and not someone else's version, especially the scrupulous mind's version. Your thoughts, memories, and judgments of yourself do not matter. What matters is that you can now recognize whether your internal experiences, if acted upon, will actually help you live the life you want to live or not. You get to decide!

Reminders

Go Beyond What You Can See

When you feel inadequate, insecure, or not good enough, remember, it's most likely because you have fallen into the scrupulosity-OCD trap.

Your journey is about personal growth and living your values. You can release fear and find peace. Your ability to apply psychological-flexibility skills will help you recognize that you no longer need to get rid of uncertainty, anxiety, or other internal experiences. You now have a more effective way to respond to your internal experiences instead of falling into the scrupulosity trap.

When you aim for living your values and acting on them, the rest falls into place.

Watch Out for Comparisons

Comparisons can strip away your joy. Your thoughts and feelings are not other people's internal experiences and behaviors. You simply cannot know what they've been through by looking at them and letting unhelpful thoughts consume you. What you see may not be reality, especially when you've become confused by the scrupulous mind.

Kind Moments

Be kinder to and more forgiving of yourself every day. You'll need those skills when you get thrown out of your boat and your mind blames it on you. There is no question we are all traveling rough waters. It is up to us to make it work. Allow others to show you kindness. They deserve to live their value of kindness. Your journey will not seem as long or hard when you practice self-compassion and rejoice in the company of loved ones.

Brave Moments

You can have brave moments even when you are afraid. When you fall out of the boat, get back in. You have tools that can help you when your boat capsizes.

Your journey with scrupulosity OCD has been arduous, yet you've been strong despite the storms you've encountered thus far. You now have the tools to keep going no matter how cloudy and stormy your travels become. As you use the tools you've been given, you'll feel empowered and confident no matter what the scrupulous mind says. You know what to do. Go live life and have brave moments!

Stay Steady During Scrupulosity Storms

Your morals, religious beliefs, and values are essential to you. Beware of the scrupulous mind twisting things around.

There will be days you just want to give up. You may experience apathy or fall prey to comparisons. Your mind may say, "Life is unfair." It may neglect to remind you that pain and suffering are universal and that ***you hurt where you care***.[2] Remember that you are not alone. We are all in the same boat, although we may experience the ride differently. It's how we respond to the ride of life that makes all the difference.

The boulders you happen upon will be big and hard. You may sometimes feel like you've been thrown out of the boat and are drowning. Don't despair. As long as you remember what matters most to you and how you will be living life (open, aware, and actively engaged), you'll be able to keep going. Those choppy waters will provide you with an opportunity to build resilience.

You don't have to get stuck in assumptions about the outcome based on previous experiences. "I always seem to quit after a great start" and "I'll never make it" are thoughts that may show up when you feel down. Your mind is a one-track *machine* looking to protect you from discomfort. Acknowledge it and keep moving toward a meaningful life.

Remember that your experiences make up your personal history and that your history is not the enemy.[3] When uncertainty and anxiety are present, thinking and talking about them is not enough. You now know how to respond by living and experiencing life as you wish and not as your overprotective, preachy, judgmental mind says you should.

In closing, I'd like to share a well-known poem that speaks to what we've learned in this workbook. Hopefully it inspires you as much as it has me.

A Psalm of Life

Tell me not, in mournful numbers,
Life is but an empty dream!
For the soul is dead that slumbers,
And things are not what they seem.

Life is real! Life is earnest!
And the grave is not its goal;
Dust thou art, to dust returnest,
Was not spoken of the soul.

Not enjoyment, and not sorrow,
Is our destined end or way;
But to act, that each to-morrow
Find us farther than to-day.

Art is long, and Time is fleeting,
And our hearts, though stout and brave,

> *Still, like muffled drums, are beating*
> *Funeral marches to the grave.*
>
> *In the world's broad field of battle,*
> *In the bivouac of Life,*
> *Be not like dumb, driven cattle!*
> *Be a hero in the strife!*
>
> *Trust no Future, howe'er pleasant!*
> *Let the dead Past bury its dead!*
> **Act—act in the living Present!**
> *Heart within, and God o'erhead!*
>
> *Lives of great men all remind us*
> *We can make our lives sublime,*
> *And, departing, leave behind us*
> *Footprints on the sands of time;*
>
> *Footprints, that perhaps another,*
> *Sailing o'er life's solemn main,*
> *A forlorn and shipwrecked brother,*
> *Seeing, shall take heart again.*
>
> **Let us, then, be up and doing,**
> *With a heart for any fate;*
> **Still achieving, still pursuing,**
> *Learn to labor and to wait.*
>
> —Henry Wadsworth Longfellow[4]

I hope you see yourself as a hero—an imperfectly good hero who has come back from being blindfolded through no fault of your own and having fallen into the scrupulosity trap. Your values, talents, and strengths make you that hero.

Live the life you deserve with resilience, hope, and peace.

Heroes believe in themselves and get back in the boat no matter how often they fall into the swirling water. You can make a powerful difference in others' lives.

You can find meaning, flexibility, and peace amid uncertainty regardless of what the scrupulous mind says.

When it starts in with its old stories, remember, you are capable of living the life you really want to live and doing what really matters most to you.

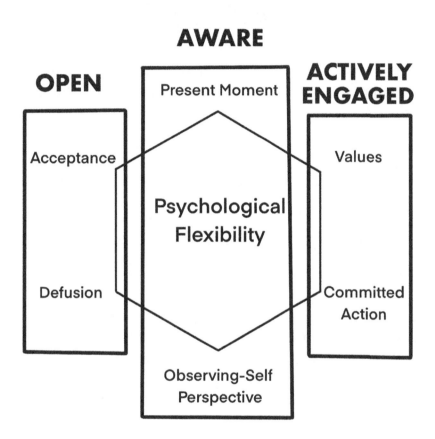

Epilogue

I'd like to invite you to write about and draw something that portrays how you view your scrupulosity OCD now that you've been practicing psychological-flexibility skills. Go back to page 34 and notice the difference and what you've learned.

This workbook is not meant to be used just once or twice. Refer to it as often as you'd like so you can continue to remind yourself how to be flexible with your internal experiences. I invite you to complete the psychological flexibility scales (next two pages) to see your progress.

The journey we are *all* on is about the process, not the outcome. Be passionate about that process!

AAQ-II

Below you will find a list of statements. Please rate how true each statement is for you by circling a number next to it. Use the scale below to make your choice.

1	2	3	4	5	6	7
never true	very seldom true	seldom true	sometimes true	frequently true	almost always true	always true

1.	My painful experiences and memories make it difficult for me to live a life that I would value.	1	2	3	4	5	6	7
2.	I'm afraid of my feelings.	1	2	3	4	5	6	7
3.	I worry about not being able to control my worries and feelings.	1	2	3	4	5	6	7
4.	My painful memories prevent me from having a fulfilling life.	1	2	3	4	5	6	7
5.	Emotions cause problems in my life.	1	2	3	4	5	6	7
6.	It seems like most people are handling their lives better than I am.	1	2	3	4	5	6	7
7.	Worries get in the way of my success.	1	2	3	4	5	6	7

Permission to print granted by Frank W. Bond

AAQ-OC

We are interested in your experiences with unwanted intrusive thoughts, ideas, impulses, doubts, images, and feelings that something is "not just right". These experiences may be bizarre, senseless, and unpleasant; they may seem inconsistent with who you are (your personality) and how you see yourself. These experiences may also seem to occur against your will; you may try hard to ignore them, but they keep coming back. Sometimes people feel the need to do something (a behavior or mental action) to try to control or remove these types of unwanted thoughts, images, or doubts in order to feel more comfortable.

The following are some examples of unwanted intrusive thoughts:
- The thought that you might have become contaminated after touching something.
- Doubts about whether or not you locked the door or turned off an appliance when you left home.
- Thoughts or urges to engage in behaviors (related to sex, immorality, or violence) that are against your morals or religious beliefs (e.g., pushing a stranger in front of oncoming traffic; a blasphemous thought).
- Thoughts or feelings that something isn't "just right" (e.g., need for symmetry).

Please note we are NOT referring to daydreams or pleasant fantasies. We are also NOT asking about depressive thoughts (e.g., "I'm worthless") or general worries about everyday matters such as money, school/work, or family issues.

Below you will find a list of statements asking about your experiences with unwanted intrusive thoughts. Please rate how true each statement is for you by selecting a number using the scale below.

1	2	3	4	5	6	7
never true	very seldom true	seldom true	sometimes true	frequently true	almost always true	always true

1. My intrusive thoughts determine the actions that I take. 1 2 3 4 5 6 7
2. I try hard to avoid having intrusive thoughts. 1 2 3 4 5 6 7
3. Intrusive thoughts get in the way of my success. 1 2 3 4 5 6 7
4. It seems like other people are handling their unwanted intrusive thoughts better than I am. 1 2 3 4 5 6 7
5. I need to control my intrusive thoughts in order to handle my life well. 1 2 3 4 5 6 7
6. I stop taking care of my responsibilities when I have intrusive thoughts. 1 2 3 4 5 6 7
7. If an unpleasant intrusive thought comes into my head, I try to get rid of it. 1 2 3 4 5 6 7
8. Intrusive thoughts cause problems in my life. 1 2 3 4 5 6 7
9. I'm afraid of my intrusive thoughts. 1 2 3 4 5 6 7
10. My intrusive thoughts prevent me from leading a fulfilling life. 1 2 3 4 5 6 7
11. I can't stand having intrusive thoughts. 1 2 3 4 5 6 7
12. I worry about not being able to control my intrusive thoughts. 1 2 3 4 5 6 7
13. I try hard to control the physical reactions that I experience in my body when I am having intrusive thoughts (e.g., heart racing, sweating). 1 2 3 4 5 6 7

Permission to print granted by Ryan Jane Jacoby

Frequently Asked Questions

- **What can I do when my public compulsions come on so fast (tic-like) I don't even realize I am doing them?**

    The connecting-to-the-present-moment practices will enhance your awareness so you can recognize the thoughts, feelings, and urges that lead to compulsions before you actually initiate them. As soon as you catch yourself giving in to a compulsion, purposely think of the distressing thought, memory, or image again. This time, instead of behaving compulsively, you can practice psychological-flexibility skills such as defusion phrases with uncertainty ("I see the thought, and, yes, I may end up acting on it. Thanks Mind!") and acceptance skills. ("I will gently hold anxiety as if it were a wounded, fragile creature.") Practicing psychological-flexibility skills is the "response prevention" part of ERP. Remember, developing awareness takes time and patience.

- **I am terrified of not feeling guilty about my intrusive thoughts because that might mean I don't care about being sinful anymore.**

    Your scrupulous mind has been telling you that you are supposed to feel guilty about your intrusive thoughts. When you fall for the mind's rigid rules, you may believe that these thoughts are equivalent to actions and facts. But you are not your thoughts and feelings. They are natural events that come and go. As you live a values-centered life, your painful internal experiences won't be your focus. Guilt may or may not be present at times. When it is, instead of trying to get rid of it, respond by using a phrase of uncertainty and allow for that guilt (openness skills). Then gently shift your focus back to the present. Remember, God knows you have OCD. Use your faith as part of your treatment.

- **I feel like an impostor when I don't give in to my usual compulsions. Is that normal?**

    Feeling like an impostor is common to all humans. However, some individuals get hooked with thoughts and feelings related to "being an impostor" more often than others. It may feel strange and stressful when you are no longer bombarded by the scrupulous mind and the unpleasant feelings you used to fight. Keep an eye on your mind when it tries to give you advice that may not be helpful. ("Something is wrong because you are not giving in to your compulsions.") Notice if you get hooked by these types of thoughts, then practice your favorite psychological-flexibility skills.

- **Sometimes I sincerely believe I am living my values, but I find myself exhausted by the end of the day. Am I going to feel this exhausted for the rest of my life?**

    You are not alone when this happens. Many people get hooked with their internal experiences and may not recognize that their "efforts" are actually compulsions. Can you allow the discomfort while engaging in what matters most rather than seeking to find relief from the uncomfortable internal events? There is no need to exhaust yourself in practicing flexibility skills. Notice if you are engaging in these skills as a way of finding relief. This mindset can lead you to exhaustion.

- **My go-to compulsion is ruminating, and I can't seem to stop it. Is it possible to eliminate this type of compulsion?**

    Many individuals find it difficult to respond effectively to this private compulsion. No worries. Implementing open and awareness skills in this workbook will allow you to notice when the scrupulous mind is providing unhelpful advice. It's best to observe and acknowledge your internal events instead of trying to stop them. As you continue to practice these skills, you may be surprised when you actually catch yourself before moving away from the present moment and what matters most.

- **How can I know if a situation is scrupulosity OCD and not a real challenge I need to deal with?**

This is a really good question. The scrupulous mind most likely will get involved in matters that are important to you. What's relevant is how you respond to your internal experiences in any situation. In trying to determine whether it is OCD or not, you most likely will get hooked by the scrupulous mind as it tries to "help" you. When you need to problem-solve, go ahead and choose to spend X amount of time on your decision by brainstorming and then writing down your options. Then advance to the present moment. Once you've made a decision, act on it and continue living a rich, values-focused life. When you are unable to make a decision and are feeling continued distress, notice what your mind is saying. Are you getting hooked by the scrupulous mind? Are you willing to feel discomfort because there is something that matters most to you? Choose the path less traveled. Notice whether your actions are in response to finding relief or if you are actually engaging in activities that move you toward living a rich and meaningful life.

- **I am not sure I can ever love myself or feel worthy of love and success. Is there any hope for me?**

    There is always hope. Your memories, thoughts, feelings, sensations, and other internal experiences are not your enemy. You don't need to believe they are permanent labels in your life. Internal experiences are like the weather. They come and go when we let them be present without doing anything about them. Respond to your internal events with flexibility. Acknowledge and allow them. Remember that you are not alone in your suffering. Others are struggling too. During difficult times, would you be willing to treat yourself as you would treat a loved one who's having a hard time? You can discover kindness is a superpower. Self-compassion can enhance your physical and mental well-being. Find out for yourself and don't ever give up.

- **I was taught that when I pray, God often answers me through my thoughts or my feelings. I just feel anxious and uncertain. What am I doing wrong?**

    Your connection to God is important. Notice if the scrupulous mind is providing rules as to what is supposed to happen or what you are supposed to feel or think. When we become rigid about our faith, we can become fused and confused. Are you willing to open up to uncertainty and anxiety? Are you willing to be open, aware, and actively engaged in what matters most to you despite the discomfort (e.g., praying and accepting that you may not feel the Holy Spirit for a while)? As you continue to practice psychological flexibility, your mind and body will become less rigid and you will find the connection with God you desire. Can you trust that the Holy Spirit knows your challenges with scrupulosity OCD? Will you trust the Holy Spirit will find a way to connect with you?

- **I have friends who show rigidity in their religious and moral beliefs but don't seem to feel anxious or guilty like I do. Why might that be so?**

    There are many people who are rigid in keeping the tenets of their religion. But they may not realize it because what they are doing is working for them at the time. Rigidity around one's religion does not necessarily mean someone has scrupulosity OCD. If they are not tormented by their thoughts, feelings, and other internal experiences, they most likely don't have the clinical condition.

- **When I write values-based scripts with uncertainty, I can't help but become sad just thinking that my core feared consequence may actually materialize. What am I doing wrong?**

    As you listen to your script and practice imaginal exposures, your mind will most likely hook you as it does at other times. The only difference is that you are purposely exhibiting a "Bring it on!" attitude so you can practice responding to the mind differently than you have (the response prevention part of the exposure). When sadness or any other feelings show up, you can give yourself the opportunity to practice openness and willingness skills. And as you do, you'll discover that you can actually change your relationship with your internal events and that you can focus on moving toward what matters most in your life. Keep living your values and doing values-based exposures every day. Remember, learning is a process.

- **No matter what I do, I cannot tolerate uncertainty. What's wrong?**

    Nothing is wrong. Your mind is always looking to keep you safe and comfortable. Feeling uncertain is not pleasant. However, your mind often fails to remind you that you actually are willing to feel uncertain in many other areas of your life. Your job is to take its advice with a grain of salt and humor it. The most traveled road might be the easy path, but it's not always the most helpful one. When you have a thought or feeling and decide to act on it, does that action move you closer to living a meaningful and values-focused life? When uncertainty shows up, continue practicing your favorite psychological-flexibility skills.

- **Your scripts are not like the scripts my therapist taught me to write. We usually write worst-case-scenario scripts. Can I write worst-case-scenario scripts too?**

    In this workbook, I chose to share values-based scripts with uncertainty, but you can use worst-case-scenario scripts with your clinician's guidance. Worst-case-scenario scripts are also effective in the treatment of OCD.

- **I can't shake the feeling of shame no matter what skills I try. Do these psychological-flexibility skills really work?**

    When we feel guilty, we feel bad about our behavior. When we feel shame, we place blame on ourselves and believe something is essentially wrong with us and that we are not worthy of love. Scrupulosity OCD can lead you to believe this is true. But shame is a universal feeling and, like other feelings, you can learn to notice and acknowledge it instead of fighting, escaping, or becoming victim to it. Be aware of getting hooked by the unhelpful advice from the mind. What matters is that you recognize this and respond differently (response prevention) than you normally would. Practice being open and willing to experience this feeling in the moment. Remember to breathe it in and create space for it. You can hold shame gently or look at it as if it were a fascinating painting. Also notice if you are using the skills as compulsions to find relief.

For more information regarding providers and treatment resources for you and your loved ones, please visit the **International OCD Foundation** website at https://iocdf.org/

You can also go to the **Faith & OCD Resource Center** page here: https://iocdf.org/faith-ocd/

To learn more about ACT and find ACT clinicians who specialize in the treatment of OCD, please visit the **Association for Contextual Behavioral Science (ACBS)** website at https://contextualscience.org/

Notes

Introduction

1. Jonathan S. Abramowitz and Joanna J. Arch, "Strategies for Improving Long-Term Outcomes in Cognitive Behavioral Therapy for Obsessive-Compulsive Disorder: Insights from Learning Theory," *Cognitive and Behavioral Practice* (February 2014), 20–31, http://dx.doi.org/10.1016/j.cbpra.2013.06.004; Michelle G. Craske, Michael Treanor, Christopher C. Conway, Tomislav Zbozinek, and Bram Vervliet, "Maximizing Exposure Therapy: An Inhibitory Learning Approach," *Behaviour Research and Therapy* (July 2014): 58, 10–23, https://doi.org/10.1016/j.brat.2014.04.006.

2. Michael P. Twohig, Jonathan S. Abramowitz, Ellen J. Bluett, Laura E. Fabricant, Ryan J. Jacoby, Kate L. Morrison, Lillian Reuman, and Brooke. M. Smith, "Exposure Therapy for OCD from an Acceptance and Commitment Therapy (ACT) Framework," *Journal of Obsessive-Compulsive and Related Disorders* 6 (July 2015): 167–73, http://dx.doi.org/10.1016/j.jocrd.2014.12.007; Michael P. Twohig, Jonathan S. Abramowitz, Brooke. M. Smith, Laura E. Fabricant, Ryan J. Jacoby, Kate L. Morrison, Ellen J. Bluett, Lillian Reuman, Shannon M. Blakey, Thomas Ledermann, "Adding Acceptance and Commitment Therapy to Exposure and Response Prevention for Obsessive-Compulsive Disorder: A Randomized Controlled Trial," *Behaviour Research Therapy* 108 (June 2018): 19, doi:10.1016/j.brat.2018.06.005, https://pubmed.ncbi.nlm.nih.gov/29966992/.

Chapter 1–Religious and Moral Anxiety: Seeing the Big Picture

Epigraph. Thomas M. Santa, *Understanding Scrupulosity: Helpful Answers for Those Who Experience Nagging Questions and Doubts*, Second Edition (Liguori, MO: Liguori/Triumph, 2007).

1. International OCD Foundation, "How to Find the Right Therapist," https://iocdf.org/ocd-finding-help/how-to-find-the-right-therapist/.

2. David L. Pauls, "The Genetics of Obsessive-Compulsive Disorder: A Review," *Dialogues in Clinical Neuroscience* 12, no. 2 (2010): 149–63, https://doi.org/10.31887/DCNS.2010.12.2/dpauls]

3. Jonathan Grayson, *Freedom from Obsessive-Compulsive Disorder: A Personalized Recovery Program for Living with Uncertainty* (Berkley Books: New York, 2004).

4. Thomas M. Santa, *Understanding Scrupulosity: Helpful Answers for Those Who Experience Nagging Questions and Doubts*, Second Edition (Liguori, MO: Liguori/Triumph, 2007).

5. Steven C. Hayes, "ACT in Practice," Praxis Continuing Education and Training, November 23, 2020–January 30, 2021.

6. Lara Boyd, "After Watching This, Your Brain Will Not Be the Same," November 2015, video, https://www.youtube.com/watch?v=LNHBMFCzznE.

7. Family Off Duty, 19 Inspiring Quotes On the Road Less Traveled, accessed November 30, 2020, https://familyoffduty.com/travel-quotes/quotes-on-the-road-less-traveled/.

8. Frank W. Bond, Steven C. Hayes, Ruth A. Baer, Kenneth M. Carpenter, Nigel Guenole, Holly K. Orcutt, Tom Waltz, & Robert D. Zettle, "Preliminary psychometric properties of the Acceptance and Action Questionnaire–II: A revised measure of psychological inflexibility and experiential avoidance." *Behavior Therapy*, (2011): 42, (4) 676-688, https://contextualscience.org/Bond_et_al_AAQ-II.

9. R. J. Jacoby, J. A. Abramowitz, J. L Buchholz, L. Reuman, & S. M. Blakey, "Experiential avoidance in the context of obsessions: Development and validation of the Acceptance and Action Questionnaire for Obsessions and Compulsions." *Journal of Obsessive Compulsive* and *Related Disorders*, (2018):19, 34-43. doi:10.1016/j.jocrd.2018.07.003, https://contextualscience.org/aaqoc_obsessions_and_compulsions.

Chapter 2–Doing What Matters Most to You

Epigraph. Trina Paulus, *Hope for the Flowers* (New York: Paulist Press, 1972).

1. Trina Paulus, *Hope for the Flowers* (New York: Paulist Press, 1972).

2. Steven C. Hayes, *Get Out of Your Mind and into Your Life* (Oakland, CA: New Harbinger, 2005).

3. Joseph V. Ciarrochi, Louise Hayes, and Ann Bailey, *Get Out of Your Mind and into Your Life for Teens: A Guide to Living an Extraordinary Life* (Oakland, CA: New Harbinger, 2012).

4. Kevin Polk, *The ACT Matrix in 13 Easy Steps*, February 7, 2015, https://www.youtube.com/playlist?list=PL6hvb2YhjnsY6vJZmeB55u53ZVPPiVNLS, video; Russ Harris, "Act with Shame, Guilt and Anger," (webinar, Contextual Consulting, June 9, 2020).

Chapter 3–Understanding the Mind

Epigraph. Daniel K. Olukoya. *MFM at 30: Milestones of God's Grace and Fire Exploits* (Lagos, Nigeria: Mountain of Fire and Miracles Ministries, 2019).

1. "Anne Morrow Lindberth Quotes," Goodreads, accessed March 21, 2021, https://www.goodreads.com/quotes/25569-i-do-not-believe-that-sheer-suffering-teaches-if-suffering.

2. Steven C. Hayes, "An Introduction to ACT as a Form of Processed Based Therapy," Suncrest Counseling, Sandy Utah, March 12–13, 2020, lecture.

3. Steven C. Hayes, *Get Out of Your Mind and into Your Life* (Oakland, CA: New Harbinger, 2005).

4. Steven C. Hayes, Kirk D. Strosahl, and Kelly G. Wilson. *Acceptance and Commitment Therapy: An Experiential Approach to Behavior Change* (New York: Guilford Press, 1999).

5. Russ Harris, *ACT Made Simple: A Quick-Start Guide to ACT Basics and Beyond* (Oakland, CA: New Harbinger, 2009).

6. Steven C. Hayes, *Get Out of Your Mind and into Your Life* (Oakland, CA: New Harbinger, 2005).

Chapter 4–Recognizing Your Internal Experiences

1. Russ Harris, *The Happiness Trap: How to Stop Struggling and Start Living* (Boston, MA: Trumpeter Books, 2008).

2. John Cloud, "Happiness Isn't Normal," *TIME*, February 2006, 167, http://search.ebscohost.com/login.aspx?direct=true&db=aph&AN=19617642&site=ehost-live.

3. Kirk Strosahl, "Focused ACT Workshop," Utah State University, April 20, 2019.

4. Kristin Neff, *Self-Compassion: The Proven Power of Being Kind to Yourself* (New York: William Morrow, 2011).

5. Kiva Botero, "Buddha's Brain: Interview with Dr. Rick Hanson on the Science and Spirituality of the Brain," *The Mindful Word*, 2012, https://www.themindfulword.org/2012/buddhas-brain-interview-rick-hanson/.

6. "Anne Frank Quotes," Goodreads, accessed March 26, 2021, https://www.goodreads.com/quotes/431935-but-feelings-can-t-be-ignored-no-matter-how-unjust-or.

7. Russ Harris, *The Happiness Trap: How to Stop Struggling and Start Living* (Boston, MA: Trumpeter Books, 2008).

8. Poetry Foundation, accessed March 4, 2021, https://www.poetryfoundation.org/poems/51642/invictus.

9. "Flexibility Quotes," accessed March 30, 2021, https://www.goodreads.com/quotes/tag/flexibility.

Chapter 5–Learning to Defuse from Your Internal Experiences

1. Russ Harris, *ACT Made Simple: A Quick-Start Guide to ACT Basics and Beyond* (Oakland, CA: New Harbinger, 2009).

2. International OCD Foundation, "Obsessions and Intrusive Thoughts Reported by Non-Clinical Samples" (Handout received from the Behavior Therapy Training Institute at Los Angeles Pasadena, California, January 27–29, 2012).

Chapter 6–Being Open to Uncertainty

1. Association for Contextual Behavioral Science, "The Magical Bank Metaphor," submitted by Dr. Claire Milligan. https://contextualscience.org/the_magical_bank_metaphor.

2. International OCD Foundation, "Distinguishing Information-Seeking and Reassurance Seeking," Developed at the Center for OCD & Anxiety Related Disorders, Saint Louis Behavioral Medicine Institute, (Handout received from the Behavior Therapy Training Institute at Los Angeles Pasadena, California, January 27–29, 2012).

Chapter 7–Taking What's Being Offered Now

Epigraph. Steven C. Hayes, *Get Out of Your Mind and into Your Life* (Oakland, CA: New Harbinger, 2005).

1. Steven C. Hayes, *A Liberated Mind: How to Pivot Toward What Matters* (New York: Avery, 2019).

2. Steven C. Hayes, *A Liberated Mind: How to Pivot Toward What Matters* (New York: Avery, 2019).

3. "Eckhart Tolle Quotes," Goodreads, accessed, March 28, 2021, https://www.goodreads.com/quotes/853487-accept---then-act-whatever-the-present-moment-contains-accept.

4. Russ Harris, *The Happiness Trap: How to Stop Struggling and Start Living* (Boston, MA: Trumpeter Books, 2008).

5. Steven C. Hayes, *A Liberated Mind: How to Pivot Toward What Matters* (New York: Avery, 2019).

Chapter 8–Addressing Dilemmas of Faith

1. "Epictetus Quotes," BrainyQuote, accessed March 4, 2019, https://www.brainyquote.com/quotes/epictetus_132944.

2. Kristin Neff, *Self-Compassion: The Proven Power of Being Kind to Yourself* (New York: William Morrow, 2011).

3. Kristin Neff, *Self-Compassion: The Proven Power of Being Kind to Yourself* (New York: William Morrow, 2011).

Chapter 9–Connecting to the Present Moment

Epigraph. Marvin J. Ashton, "The Time is Now," *Ensign*, May 1975.

1. Minda Zetlin, "Constant Multitasking Is Damaging Millennial Brains, Research Shows," *Inc.*, July 30, 2016, https://www.inc.com/minda-zetlin/constant-multitasking-is-damaging-millennial-brains-research-shows.html; see also Nancy K. Napier, "The Myth of Multitasking," *Psychology Today*, May 12, 2014, https://www.psychologytoday.com/us/blog/creativity-without-borders/201405/the-myth-multitasking.

2. Russ Harris, *The Happiness Trap: How To Stop Struggling and Start Living* (Boston, MA: Trumpeter Books, 2008).

3. Steven C. Hayes, *A Liberated Mind: How to Pivot Toward What Matters* (New York: Avery, 2019).

4. "Viktor E. Frankl Quotes," BrainyQuote, accessed May 27, 2021, https://www.brainyquote.com/quotes/viktor_e_frankl_160380.

5. "Mindful Eating," *Harvard Health Letter*, February 2011, https://www.health.harvard.edu/staying-healthy/mindful-eating.

6. Hank Robb, in Jason A. Nieuwsma, Robyn D. Walser, Steven C. Hayes, eds. *Act for Clergy and Pastoral Counselors: Using Acceptance and Commitment Therapy* (Oakland, CA: New Harbinger, 2016), 87.

Chapter 10—Being Aware of Being Aware

Epigraph. Steven C. Hayes, *A Liberated Mind: How to Pivot Toward What Matters* (New York: Avery, 2019).

1. "Jon Kabat-Zinn Quotes," BrainyQuotes, accessed March 12, 2021, https://www.brainyquote.com/quotes/jon_kabatzinn_637563.

2. Steven C. Hayes, *A Liberated Mind: How to Pivot Toward What Matters* (New York: Avery, 2019).

3. Adapted from ACT: Anxiety, Tom Lavin interview with Steven C. Hayes, accessed February 15, 202, https://www.youtube.com/watch?v=XWc8OoGK8v8.

Chapter 11—Developing Self-Forgiveness and Self-Compassion

Epigraph. Asad Meah, "35 Inspirational Quotes on Self-Forgiveness." Awaken the Greatness Within, October, 2018, https://www.awakenthegreatnesswithin.com/35-inspirational-quotes-on-self-forgiveness/.

1. Steven C. Hayes, *Get Out of Your Mind and into Your Life* (Oakland, CA: New Harbinger, 2005).

2. Steven C. Hayes, "An Introduction to ACT as a Form of Processed Based Therapy," Suncrest Counseling, Sandy Utah, March 12–13, 2020, lecture.

3. Sue C. Bratton, Garry L. Landreth, Theresa Kellam, and Sandra R. Blackard, *Child Parent Relationship Therapy (CRT) Treatment Manual: A 10-Session Filial Therapy Model for Training Parents* (New York: Routledge, 2006).

4. "Henri Nouwen Quotes and Sayings," *inspiringquotes*, accessed, March 3, 2021, https://www.inspiringquotes.us/author/3299-henri-nouwen.

5. Steven C. Hayes, *Mental Brakes to Avoid Mental Breaks*, Ted Talks, July 2016, https://www.youtube.com/watch?v=GnSHpBRLJrQ, YouTube video file.

6. Steven C. Hayes, *A Liberated Mind: How to Pivot Toward What Matters* (New York: Avery, 2019).

7. Steven C. Hayes, *A Liberated Mind: How to Pivot Toward What Matters* (New York: Avery, 2019).

8. Steven C. Hayes, "An Introduction to ACT as a Form of Processed Based Therapy," Suncrest Counseling, Sandy Utah, March 12–13, 2020, lecture.

9. "Jack Kornfield Quotes," Goodreads, accessed February 28, 2021, https://www.goodreads.com/quotes/41119-if-your-compassion-does-not-include-yourself-it-is-incomplete.

10. Kristin Neff, *Self-Compassion: The Proven Power of Being Kind to Yourself* (New York: William Morrow, 2011).

11. Kristin Neff, *Self-Compassion: The Proven Power of Being Kind to Yourself* (New York: William Morrow, 2011).

12. Kristin Neff, *Self-Compassion: The Proven Power of Being Kind to Yourself* (New York: William Morrow, 2011).

13. Marianne Williamson, *A Return to Love: Reflections on the Principles of a Course in Miracles* (New York: HarperOne, 1992).

Chapter 12–Staying on the Path Less Traveled

1. Adapted from Joyce C. Mills, "Reconnecting to the Magic of Life," *Kekaha* (Kaua'i, HI: Imaginal Press, 1999).

Chapter 13–Being Willing to Do What It Takes

1. Steven C. Hayes, *Get Out of Your Mind and into Your Life* (Oakland, CA: New Harbinger, 2005).

2. Michael P. Twohig, Jonathan S. Abramowitz, Ellen J. Bluett, Laura E. Fabricant, Ryan J. Jacoby, Kate L. Morrison, Lillian Reuman, Brooke M. Smith, "Exposure Therapy for OCD from an Acceptance and Commitment Therapy (ACT) Framework," *Journal of Obsessive-Compulsive and Related Disorders* 6 (July 2015): 167–73, https://doi.org/10.1016/j.jocrd.2014.12.007.

3. Kristin Neff and Christopher Germer, *The Mindful Self-Compassion Workbook: A Proven Way to Accept Yourself, Build Inner Strength, and Thrive* (New York: The Guilford Press, 2018).

Chapter 14–Stepping into the River

Epigraph. "John C. Maxwell Quotes," Goodreads, accessed March 29, 2021, https://www.goodreads.com/quotes/81497-change-is-inevitable-growth-is-optional.

1. Jonathan S. Abramowitz, Brett J. Deacon, and Stephen P. H. Whiteside, *Exposure Therapy for Anxiety: Principles and Practice*, Second Edition (New York: The Guilford Press, 2019).

2. "Tony Robbins Quotes," "Quotefancy, accessed April 8, 2021, https://quotefancy.com/quote/922750/Tony-Robbins-All-growth-starts-at-the-end-of-your-comfort-zone.

3. Jonathan S. Abramowitz, Brett J. Deacon, and Stephen P. H. Whiteside, *Exposure Therapy for Anxiety: Principles and Practice*, Second Edition (New York: The Guilford Press, 2019).

Chapter 15–Going Beyond What You See

1. Directed by Roger Allers and Robert Minkoff (United States: Walt Disney Productions, 1994), motion picture.

2. Steven C. Hayes, "An Introduction to ACT as a Form of Processed Based Therapy," Suncrest Counseling, Sandy Utah, March 12–13, 2020, lecture.

3. John Cloud, "Happiness Isn't Normal," *TIME*, February 2006, 167, http://search.ebscohost.com/login.aspx?direct=true&db=aph&AN=19617642&site=ehost-live.

4. Henry Wadsworth Longfellow. Poetry Foundation, accessed April 8, 2021, https://www.poetryfoundation.org/poems/44644/a-psalm-of-life.

Note to the Reader

Thank you so much for taking the time to read this workbook. I hope it resonates with you and inspires you to keep going on the path less traveled and that you can do it with meaning, flexibility and peace. If you've found even a small part of this read beneficial, it would mean a great deal to me if you could leave a review on wherever you bought this—and, of course, spread the word!

What's Next?

I hope you will continue to refer back to this workbook often so you can continue to move toward what matters most in your life every day. You can also visit my website at mindsetfamilytherapy.com and sign up for free downloads such as:

- "Mindful Conversations"
- "Refraining from Compulsions through Writing"
- "Walking through the Library Halls"

You can also sign up for my monthly newsletter and receive evidence-based skills to help you keep moving toward your values and continue to live with meaning, flexibility, and peace regardless of what the scrupulous mind says.

About the Author

Annabella Hagen is the clinical director and founder of Mindset Family Therapy in Provo, Utah. Her focus is on working with clients who suffer from anxiety, OCD, and OC-spectrum disorders. She is passionate about ACT. She loves to see her clients progress as they fully engage in their treatment and experience the journey back to living a values-centered life.

Annabella obtained her MSW degree from Brigham Young University. She is a member of the International OCD Foundation and the Association for Contextual Behavioral Science. She is regular presenter for the International OCD Foundation's yearly conferences.

Annabella is the author of two children's books, *Emma's Worry Clouds* and *Nico the Worried Caterpillar*. She is also author of *Let Go of Anxiety: Climb Life's Mountains with Peace, Purpose, and Resilience* and coauthor of the parenting book *The Masterpiece Mindset*. She writes for various online magazines and her business blog. She enjoys walking, classical music, reading, yoga, and finding new adventures when she travels. Her favorite pastime is playing with her grandchildren.

Made in United States
North Haven, CT
09 April 2024